EATING FOR EXCELLENCE
Cookbook

Sheri Rose Shepherd

Multnomah Publishers® *Sisters, Oregon*

EATING FOR EXCELLENCE

published by Multnomah Publishers, Inc.

© 1999 by Sheri Rose Shepherd

International Standard Book Number: 1-57673-487-0

Design by Stephen Gardner

Cover photos by Mike Houska

Interior illustrations by Elizabeth Haidle

Back cover illustration by Daniel Adel

Scripture quotations are from

The Holy Bible, New International Version © 1973, 1984

by International Bible Society, used by permission of Zondervan Publishing House

Multnomah is a registered trademark of Multnomah Publishers, Inc.,

and is registered in the U.S. Patent and Trademark Office.

The colophon is a trademark of Multnomah Publishers, Inc.

Printed in the United States of America

For information:

MULTNOMAH PUBLISHERS, INC.

POST OFFICE BOX 1720

SISTERS, OREGON 97759

99 00 01 02 03 04 05 06 — 10 9 8 7 6 5 4 3 2 1

Contents

Acknowledgments

*"For I know the plans I have for
you," declares the LORD, "plans to prosper
you and not to harm you,
plans to give you hope and a future."*
—Jeremiah 29:11

I want to thank the precious people who have been a part of God's plan for my life: To all the wonderful staff at Multnomah Publishers and especially Don and Matt Jacobson, thank you for believing in me enough to birth an author. To Duane and LeeAnn Rawlins, thank you for your hearts of gold and your words of wisdom. To my stepmom, Susie Goodman, for taking me from my worst and helping me to be my best (God knows that's a major job!). Thank you so much for creating and sharing all your original recipes in this book.

To my father, Phil Goodman, who has given me the courage to say and ask for anything. To my mother, Carole Goodman, for the timely, tender words of truth that helped set me free from my past.

To my office assistants, Tanna Behling, Lana Krug, Chera Hicks, and Rochelle Pederson, thanks for making this message possible through your incredible gifts of organization and service. To Carol DeKorte, for typing this manuscript on a moment's notice, and to Jennifer Curley and Zoë Tennesen, for your proofreading and editing skills. And of course, Steve Gardner for your hard work and creative design and Elizabeth Haidle, for your wonderful cartoons.

To my handsome husband, Steven, for learning to live in my world and for loving me through my dangerous dreams. To my precious son, Jacob Andrew, for the joy you bring to my heart.

And to God, for loving me just the way I am, yet loving me too much to leave me this way.

Introduction

I used to travel through life in two gears: *park* and *fifth*. I pushed myself to the highest speed limits possible, ignoring the big yellow warning lights telling me, "Slow down! Rest! Severe exhaustion ahead."

I was so consumed with getting to my destination of the day, completing my unrealistic to-do list, that I didn't hear my body's cry for wellness. I was living life in fast-forward, and when I didn't think I could handle traveling one more mile at this speed, I pushed down the pedal even harder. I thought the Scripture that says, "The spirit is willing but the flesh is weak" meant it's okay and even spiritual to ignore your body's need for rest, replenishment, relaxation, and restoration.

The next thing I knew, I experienced a crash and was thrown out onto the road of reality. There I was, speaking to a group of ladies on spiritual excellence, when I collapsed onto the floor. This was not a spiritual experience; I mean, I totally blacked out. That evening I was taken to the hospital and was diagnosed with Epstein-Barr virus, more commonly known as chronic fatigue syndrome. My immune system had completely shut down, and I was so exhausted I couldn't lift my head off the pillow. The doctor told me I would have to stop all activity. Shut down. In other words, pull my lifestyle out of fifth gear and put it in park, indefinitely.

There I lay, face to face with the fear that I might never regain my health and energy. I didn't have the strength to clean my house, play with my little boy, go to church, or visit with friends. Although many people were praying for me, my chronic fatigue grew worse. The word *health* took on a much more significant meaning to me. Up to this point, I had always been able to push myself through any obstacles that got in the way of my goals: I had overcome the pain of growing up in a dysfunctional home; God delivered me from drug addiction; I had been healed from an eating disorder; and I lost more than sixty pounds and had kept it off for over seventeen years. I started out in school as a dyslexic D-student and ended up an author and public speaker.

This was the first thing that seemed completely out of my control. After weeks of lying in bed, depressed and sick, I begged God to show me his plan to help me regain my health and energy. Through much prayer, research, and study, I learned that sickness and exhaustion are our body's warning lights—they're God-given sensors that tell us something needs attention in our bodies.

I've learned it's choice, not chance, that creates an excellent life. We can choose the *easy* way—or the *excellent* way. There will always be a battle between the mind-set of mediocrity and the spirit of excellence. However, there is something deep down inside us that craves excellence (even more than chocolate!). *Eating for Excellence* is designed to show you the excellent way. If you're ready to lose weight and regain your energy, let's begin our journey together. May God give you the wisdom to understand the truths written in this book and the strength to follow the plan that's right for you. Once you start, don't look back—remember, failure is not final. This is a new day and a new way, created especially for you.

Chapter 1

Eat at Your Own Risk

Where is the lifeguard to save us from the sea of sickness? To keep us from drowning in the pool of bloating or rescue us from the river of exhaustion? Or maybe I should ask, where is the *mouthguard* to protect us from eating poisonous chemicals, bleached sugars, saturated fats, and drugs cleverly disguised as food?

If you're exhausted and praying for God to give you enough energy for the day, I want to assure you that God hears your cry for wellness. He is the Great Physician, but we must choose to follow his prescription for wellness. He loves us too much to reward us for traveling down the wrong road to recovery. His love is unconditional, but his promises are not. First Corinthians 3:16–17 says, "Don't you know that you yourselves are God's temple and that God's Spirit lives in you? If anyone destroys God's temple, God will destroy him; for God's temple is sacred, and you are that temple." We won't experience good health and energy if we make God's temple our trash can.

Most of us are likely to miss out on the power of the biblical word picture found in the above verse. Today temples have no real significance; but to God's chosen people, the temple was the lifeblood of the civilization. It was the source of power, direction, and protection. It was the most beautifully designed, painstakingly immaculate, awe-inspiring fixture in the entire culture. It was functional, holy, and artistic all in one. Why would God use this spectacular man-made creation as a symbol for our earthly body? Because both are his chosen place of dwelling. Romans 12:1 tells us we are therefore to present our bodies as a living and holy sacrifice to God.

Maybe these ideas of *sacrifices* and *temples* are foreign to you. I was raised Jewish, and I remember learning at a young age that a sacrifice should be something of value, something pure, something set apart for a special purpose. When I was younger, I never felt that way about myself. I didn't recognize the value that God had given me. I also didn't realize the tragic consequences of my ignorance.

Many people today suffer from the same tragic lack of knowledge. They have no idea that they are putting processed drugs and chemicals into their bodies every meal they eat. They are slowly poisoning themselves, yet they have turned a deaf ear to their bodies as they murmur, "Exhaustion. Sickness. Bloating. Headache. Fat. Help!" If they do not listen, their bodies talk louder by crying, "Breakdown! I can't take any more!" At that point, chronic, degenerative, and perhaps even fatal disease eventually wins the war over their health.

This is not God's will for your life. Our lives were designed somewhat like a tricycle. The big wheel in the front is the spiritual wheel that guides, directs, and keeps us on course. But to ride with total health and harmony, we must also pay attention to the back wheels. They provide critical balance that keeps us out of the gutter. One wheel is our mind (our intellect) and the other is our physical body. All three wheels must work in unison to stay on the road toward excellence.

A healthy lifestyle is not about denial; it's about desire. It wasn't until I gave up the foods that were destroying my body that God blessed me with renewed health and energy. Ask yourself the following questions: Is it worth giving up unhealthy foods to answer my body's cry and God's will for me to enjoy good health? Which wheel in my life am I neglecting? Or rather, which wheel is distracting me from living to the fullest? In the book of Daniel, the young prophet knew that eating daily of the king's delicacies would detour him from God's direction for his life. Daniel and his friends took the excellent way, and God blessed them with extra strength, wisdom, and favor (see Daniel 1).

This chapter lists what I call Life Safety Rules, which reveal the main foods and substances that keep us locked up in an unhealthy prison of poison. The Life Safety Rules also teach what will make our bodies healthy, fit, and alive. Remember, listen to the lifeguard—your body's voice. By facing these food facts and applying them, you'll be on the right road to wellness. Following this road could even save your life.

Life Safety Rule 1:   STOP BUYING LIES

When you sit to dine with a ruler,
note well what is before you,
and put a knife to your throat
if you are given to gluttony.
Do not crave his delicacies,
for that food is deceptive.
                    Proverbs 23:1–3

Are we being deceived? The food industry makes billions of dollars each year from our ignorance. Somehow, their marketing magic has made us feel safe eating foods labeled *fat free, sugar free,* and *artificial flavor.* How safe are we? I learned through research that most of the artificially enhanced, beautifully packaged, overprocessed foods we buy aren't really even food at all. In many cases, the packaging would be safer to eat than the food inside. *Fast food* is a perfect title, because it's better to fast than to eat it!

Think about how you feel when you ingest these substances. Eat one of these foods on an empty stomach, wait twenty minutes, and then let your body tell you whether that food is right for you. Eating these toxic foods on a regular basis can have a lasting effect on your health. Try answering the following questions:

Do you feel well?
Are you exhausted much of the time?
Do you get headaches?
Do you wake up tired?
Is your skin dull or washed out?
Do you have digestive problems?

If you answered yes to any of these questions, I want to encourage you to listen to your body. It's not too late to make healthy choices. In fact, starting to make the right choices now could change your life. Look at these alarming facts about the state of Americans' health:

Fact: 1 in 3 of us will develop cancer.
Fact: Cancer is now killing more children between the ages of 3 and 14 than any other cause of death.
Fact: 1 million of us will die from heart disease this year.
Fact: Millions suffer from chronic fatigue syndrome.
Fact: Despite our preoccupation with health and fitness, we as a nation are becoming more obese and dangerously unhealthy.

"Be not deceived: God cannot be mocked. A man reaps what he sows" (Galatians 6:7). We are certainly reaping the effects of poor nutrition, lack of exercise, sleep deprivation, and ignorance. Our former surgeon general, C. Everett Koop, said 70 percent of all premature deaths can be attributed to improper nutrition. He and some 250 scientists published a report that linked diet with our society's most widespread diseases: cancer, diabetes, stroke, and heart disease. Before artificial food, chemicals, and drugs were introduced to our food supply, heart disease and cancer were almost nonexistent.

What happened? Who told us these things were safe? And if we continue to believe and buy these lies, what will it cost to buy our health back? Billions of dollars are spent each year in cancer recovery and heart surgeries. Let's count the cost and buy real food.

Warning: The following information, when applied, has been known to turn couch potatoes into hot tomatoes. So if you're down and out (pooped out, that is), this may be just what you need to get ready to shout victory over exhaustion.

☞ Life Safety Rule 2 : **START DRINKING**

I'm serious. First thing in the morning, drink a huge glass of purified water on an empty stomach. I realize the water doesn't smell like your coffee, but it's a sweet aroma to your body's engine. Water puts oxygen into your blood and the blood brings oxygen to your brain. It cleans out your colon, flushes out fat, relieves water retention, creates beautiful skin, gives you more energy, removes toxins from your body, and is essential to your health.

Our bodies require a minimum of 6 to 8 glasses of purified water (not tap water, which usually contains chlorine) per day. Don't assume that you can drink coffee, tea, or soda as a substitute. These fluids will actually dehydrate you. Most people only drink 1 to 2 glasses of water per day. Believe it or not, as a nation we actually consume more soft drinks than we do water. Just remember, when you wake up, start drinking and continue drinking throughout the day and you'll swim through life like a champion.

☞ Life Safety Rule 3 : **SUCK SOME AIR**

This is the most vital life safety rule of all. We can live forty days without food, four days without water, but we will die in four minutes without oxygen.

Okay, so you're breathing now—without even trying. But I'm talking about more than just breathing. Exercise is essential to get oxygen to your cells. God created us to be physically active. Before remote controls, telephones, computers, and cars, men and women walked many miles a day.

Oxygen brings life to your body. This concept was proved in the Garden of Eden when God blew the breath of life into Adam's nose. Some of us desperately need to learn to breathe deep. I've seen people who are so stressed they look as if their air supply has been cut off. Not only does oxygen help your body burn fat, it is the very essence of life. So let's suck some air.

Read the following facts about oxygen and see if they aren't enough to make you want to work your lungs:

Oxygen...
detoxifies our blood
strengthens our immune system
heightens concentration and alertness
rejuvenates and revitalizes unhealthy cells
slows down the aging process
helps depression

If you're bored with traditional exercises like jogging, aerobics classes, and exercise machines, here are some fun and creative ways to help firm and exercise your body: 1) Stop using garbage bags and take your trash out one piece at a time. 2) Kick all your bathwater out of the tub rather than using the drain. 3) Go grocery shopping without a cart. Or fill your cart to the brim with the heaviest jumbo-size canned goods you can find and take a few quick laps around the store. 4) To firm your upper body, dramatically lift your elbows up and down while brushing your teeth. 5) Tell your hair-stylist you'd like a little off the top and your bottom—and insist that the chair won't be necessary; squatting is excellent for the buns. 6) Hug your loved ones really tight for 10 to 15 minutes (in-laws sometimes require more). 7) To work your lips, an armful of grandchildren is plenty of exercise. 8) Stretch your neck in a restaurant when you want to hear what's going on in the booth next to you, then wrap it up by chasing down your waiter to get the bill.

Remember to try to make exercise fun. All kidding aside, we will not enjoy a long, excellent life without it.

☞ Life Safety Rule 4: **TURN GREEN**

When we're at a stoplight, we don't go until the light turns green. Many of us are so tired, we drive through the red and the yellow lights, never experiencing the green light of life.

Here are some ways to turn your green light on: Eat dark green, leafy veggies in the raw, especially for lunch. Fresh vegetables have an alkaline effect on the body (as opposed to the acidic effect of animal products; some studies have shown that an alkaline environment inhibits the growth of cancer). And the fact is, live food makes you feel alive and dead food makes you feel like walking death.

Another green light of life is Barley Green Powder. I conquered chronic fatigue syndrome when I introduced my body to a morning and afternoon Barley Green drink. Okay, I'll admit that at first I thought it tasted like the bottom of a lawn mower, but once I experienced the powerful effects it had on my body, I became addicted to the Green fix. For people who can't handle the taste of lawn, the good news is that Barley Green comes in tablets (however, the powder assimilates faster and more effectively).

Life Safety Rule 5: DON'T BE SO SWEET!

Yes, I am talking about the *S* word. I admit that those sugary treats taste like heaven going down, but they torment our bodies while passing through. Think about what happens to a car when someone puts sugar in the gas tank: it kills the engine. Our bodies react in a similar way.

Believe it or not, sugar should be labeled "legal drug." If you doubt this, try to stop. Our bodies actually go into a state of detoxification, with withdrawal symptoms similar to what an alcoholic experiences giving up alcohol. God created the natural form of sugar found in raw fruits, raw vegetables, and honey. It's safe and provides fuel for the cells of the body. But man stepped in and "enhanced" God's sugar by using fourteen steps to process sugarcane and sugar beets to make sucrose.

Bleached white sugar has a toxic, drugging effect on the body. Even in small doses, it causes the immune system's capability to decrease by as much as 50 percent. When it enters the bloodstream, it takes on the forms of carbonic acid, acetic acid, and alcohol. Acetic acid literally burns up our cells.

Sugar has been known to contribute to depression, fatigue, irritability, hypoglycemia, diabetes, hyperactivity, and violent outrages. A study was done in a mental hospital in which the patients had all bleached white sugar and bleached white flour removed from their diets. Within thirty days, 50 percent of the patients had their mental health restored.

Renowned doctors such as Dr. Linus Pauling, Dr. A. Hoffer, Dr. Allan Kott, and Dr. A. Cherkin have confirmed that emotional disturbances can be merely the first symptom of the obvious inability of the human system to handle the stress of sugar dependency. The average American consumes 120 pounds a year of this sweet white stuff, and unfortunately, we're usually addicted to sugar as infants before we ever get home from the hospital (bottled sugar water is the beverage of choice by hospitals).

The good news is that we can kick the habit. As we wean ourselves from sugary foods and drinks, our taste buds become retrained, and our overindulged cravings for sweets diminish. I'm not saying you should never eat sugar again (I still eat it once in a while); I am saying if we're going to eat for excellence, we will have to stop being so sweet.

(For more research about the effects of sugar, read *Sugar Blues* by William Dufty, published by Warner Books.)

✋ Life Safety Rule 6 : **DON'T BE SO FAKE**

Just when you're ready to kick your sugar habit and dive into your sugar-free sodas, cakes, and cookies, I had to ruin it for you with Life Safety Rule #6. I hate being the party pooper, but it's only fair to tell you the whole truth: So let's talk artificial, artificial sweeteners; there's only one thing worse than being too sweet, and that's being fake!

Somehow we've bought the lie that artificial sweeteners are safe and a better alternative to sugar. Dr. Russell L. Blaylock, a professor of neurosurgery at the Medical University of Mississippi, recently published a book thoroughly detailing the severe damage that is caused when aspartic acid from aspartame is ingested. Blaylock uses over 500 scientific studies that expose these harmful effects, such as seizures, schizophrenia, Alzheimer's disease, and even death.

In 1981, Satya Dubey, an FDA statistician, stated that the brain tumor data related to consuming aspartame was so worrisome that he could not recommend the approval of Nutrasweet. He felt the approval of aspartame was a violation of the Delaney Amendment, which was legislated to prevent cancer-causing substances from entering our food supply. What's even more interesting is that the FDA gets more complaints about aspartame than any other substance on the market. Some of the complaints include migraine headaches, dizziness, memory loss, severe abdominal pains, nausea, depression, breathing problems, and fatigue. This artificial "guilt-free fix" is affecting an enormous number of people without their realization. The food fact is that if we're going to eat for excellence, we're going to stop being so fake and get real! (Check out the Internet for more information on the affects of aspartame.)

✋ Life Safety Rule 7 :   STOP MILKING THE COW

Who taught us that dairy is the magic fairy that keeps us healthy? It's interesting to know that the Meat and Dairy Association designed the four basic food groups we studied in school. What a great way to keep us *mooing* for more dairy when we're adults. Speaking of grown-ups, we humans are the only species that continues to drink milk as adults. Even baby cows stop drinking milk. After all, milk was designed to turn an 80-pound calf into a 600-pound cow!

What keeps us mooing for more? I bet you're thinking, I need my calcium. Do you know that green leafy vegetables have more digestible calcium than milk? As a matter of fact, milk has so much concentrated protein in it that studies show it's almost impossible to assimilate the calcium. Meat and dairy also become very acidic in the body when they are digested, and cancer thrives in that type of environment. Some more food for thought: if you suffer from allergies, breathing difficulties, digestion problems, or acne, try weaning yourself off the cow and see what happens.

Remember, the lifeguard is your body's voice. Let your body tell you how much dairy you should eat. There are terrific alternatives that make your body strong and your taste buds happy (see the shopping list in chapter 4).

✋ Life Safety Rule 8 : STOP EATING BLEACH WITH YOUR BREAD

Do you know what our food manufacturers are doing with our pasty white flour? It's time to swallow another food fact, so get ready.

First, they take beautiful brown whole grain designed by God to nourish and flourish our bodies, and they remove all the wheat germ and bran. Then they bleach it white with chemicals similar to Clorox bleach. To add insult to injury, they then sell the wheat germ and bran back to us and call it health food!

Check the package when you buy your flour. Unless the label states "unbleached," I'm sad to say that you'll be ingesting bleach with your bread. So read the labels, get rid of the chemicals, and get ready to eat for excellence!

✋ Life Safety Rule 9 : STOP RUNNING ON EMPTY

I saved this Life Safety Rule until now because I didn't want you to completely break down when we cut back your caffeine supply. A cup a day may keep depression away, but a pot a day will take your health away.

If we run on iced tea, coffee, and cola fixes all day, our bodies develop deficient-B disorder. *B* as in kiss your B vitamins good-bye and say hello to stress, nervousness, breast lumps, and headaches. Coffee is not a food; it is a drug that contains caffeine along with harmful oils and other toxic substances. It contributes to mental depression and nerve exhaustion; it damages the liver; it raises blood pressure and causes the kidneys to work overtime in an effort to get rid of this poison. Because coffee's poisoning effects to the body have a slow effect, most of us don't notice it until it's too late.

For many of us, our consumption of coffee is just a cover-up for a deeper problem: we do not get enough rest. Our nation suffers from sleep deprivation. Our bodies cannot rebuild or replenish without proper rest. Many of us short-circuit the natural plan for rest by ingesting substances that are intended to artificially stimulate. If we're going to eat for excellence, we're going to have to cut back our caffeine supply...and get some rest!

Life Safety Rule 10 : TRASH IT BEFORE IT TRASHES YOU

No one likes to take out the trash, but we feel much better when it's gone. Just like cleaning out our houses, it's important to clean out our bodies. To experience excellence in our health, we must remove the toxins stored in our bodies.

We spend years trashing our bodies, but fortunately it takes only 5 to 30 days to reverse the curse, depending on how severe the internal damage is. For some that detoxification time can feel like eternity. You may experience headaches and flulike symptoms; to speed up the detoxification process, increase your water and fiber intake. After the toxins are removed, you will experience a euphoric feeling of wellness unlike anything you've ever known. The whites of your eyes will be whiter, your skin will glow, your mind will feel clear, your energy level will increase, and you'll begin to enjoy life the way God intended you to.

The first step to detoxifying your body is to throw away everything in your kitchen cupboards and refrigerator that is fake food. White sugar, bleached white flour, soft drinks. Don't say you don't want to waste money by getting rid of so much food. *It will cost much more to buy back your health if you continue to eat this toxic food.*

If you have a family, don't announce out loud that you're throwing away their goodies. This could be more hazardous to your health than the toxic food. Slowly begin to introduce more fresh foods into the meals. If you have dessert recipes they love, then switch the white flour to organic wheat flour or barley flour. Switch the white sugar to birch sugar or honey. Remember, this is *not* a diet—it's a new way of life.

Chapter 2

Fat Busters

I recently saw a bumper sticker that read, *Lord, if I can't be thin, make all my friends fat.*

Have you ever thought about how much time and money we women spend on our fat? We spend money to exercise our fat, cover our fat, tan our fat, and suck our fat. We buy books and magazines to read about our fat. We buy pills to try to dissolve our fat. We enroll in classes to learn more about our fat. No wonder our fat doesn't go away. Would you go away if someone spent that much time and money on you?

It seems as if we're in a constant battle with our bulges. However, our fat does create a special bonding between us women. I mean, have you ever noticed that when a group of us get together the topic of conversation is usually fat, PMS, bloating, sickness, or exhaustion? As we begin to eat for excellence, we also have to work on creating new topics to talk about. No matter how much we joke about it, the truth is that deep down inside each of us is a desire to be healthy and thin. The proof is in the billions of dollars we spend each year on diets, exercise programs, and gimmicks that promise perfection without effort.

Let me take you back to the Kodak moment that changed the course of my life and gave me a radical reality check. There I sat, posed in front of the camera, proud as I could be because I had stuck to a healthy, low-fat diet for over twenty-four hours. I wanted my stepmom, Susie, to shoot me (with a camera, that is). She tried to warn me to wait a few weeks to take the photo, but I said, "I feel thin enough today to suck in, so take the photo before I pass out!"

Have you ever heard the saying "A picture is worth a thousand words"? This picture left me speechless, which is almost impossible to do. I'll never forget the way I felt when I saw my "before" photo. I was shocked to see my body covered in all that excess fat, and as I sat there staring at myself, I burst into tears. My stepmom said tenderly, "We're going to uncover that thin healthy body inside of you together by eating for excellence." And that was where it all started.

I used to have an intense love affair with food. My taste buds didn't know how to read ingredients. My definition of cutting calories was "stop licking the plate." When I went out to eat, I stuffed myself until I was completely full—and then I'd order dessert. I ate one meal a day: it started in the morning and ended when I fell asleep. I used to think of myself as a light eater, because I started eating as soon as it was light. I was what society refers to as a food addict. I purposely didn't keep track of my menstrual cycle so I would always have a PMS excuse when my eating was out of control. As a matter of fact, I made up a new meaning for the acronym PMS: Pass More Sugar.

I used and abused food for years. It started when I was a little girl. I used to dig out the entire center of a loaf of Wonder white bread and roll it up into a big ball of paste so it appeared smaller than a loaf. Then I'd quickly stuff it into my mouth. I knew all kinds of tricks to hide my food addiction. At holidays, when the ten-pound box of chocolates was set out on the coffee table, I would take out each piece, dig out the center with my fingernail, then strategically put it back into the box for others to enjoy the empty shell of chocolate. When I was a teenager I landed a food addict's dream job—I was a spy for a fast-food hot-dog chain. I got paid to eat fatty foods, and I took my job seriously. I didn't eat to live, I lived to eat! Once I was so hungry during a family barbecue that I ran right through the screen door to get to the food. Believe it or not, I was so focused on the food that I didn't see the screen.

Today, I'm free from my food addiction. I still love to eat—but now that I eat for excellence, life means more to me than a box of chocolates. I know that overcoming a weight problem can be a long, hard battle, and if you need help with a similar problem, I want to help you by sharing what I've learned. The following Fat Busters are what helped me to finally win the war with my weight:

Fat Buster 1: PRAY

It might seem strange to ask God to help us eat right and lose weight. But God's Word promises that he will be strong in our weakness. I think most of us fail to accomplish our goals of weight loss because we try to do it in our own strength.

I'm weak in the food department, so every morning I ask my heavenly Father to bring some order to my day; to give me wisdom to know what to eat and give me the strength to walk away from tempting foods that will make me fat, tired, and depressed. By doing this I allow the spirit of God to give me self-control, which is fruit of the Spirit. The Bible tells us we have not because we ask not. Ask God to help you every day.

Fat Buster 2: DO IT THE RIGHT WAY FOR THE RIGHT REASONS

If we're dieting to look like Barbies with a Bible, then we've already failed. Sure, there are many physical benefits to eating for excellence. But more important than the outer appearance are the benefits of a healthy mind and the energy to allow your soul to prosper. I think of my diet as a sacrifice to God: I want to give up the foods that destroy my body (his temple) because he gave up his life for me.

And remember, people in many other countries have little or no choice in what they eat—it's a privilege to have the choice to eat right.

Fat Buster 3 : DON'T DO IT ALONE

Accountability is the key. Very rarely do you see success without accountability. I now have more accountability than I'd like as a result of writing this book. Every meal I eat, people watch me eat. Sometimes I want to run into a bathroom stall and eat twenty Twinkies. But most of the time I'm thankful for those watching me, because accountability keeps me faithful to do what I know is right.

So tell your friends, coworkers, and family you have made a commitment to yourself and to God to give up junk food. Then ask one particular person (not your husband) to help you keep your commitment.

Fat Buster 4 : PREPARE FOR EXCELLENCE

We will not win the war with our weight if we are not prepared. Because of our busy lifestyles, very few of us have the time or energy to prepare fresh, healthy food every day. By taking one day each week to prepare ahead, you can save time when you're too busy or tired to fix three meals a day. Try the following tasks to help you fight the battle of the bulge:

- Select your menus from the recipes in this book. Write out your choices and make a trip to the grocery store and health food store to purchase everything you need.
- Cut up lots of different raw veggies. Put them in Ziploc bags and store them in the refrigerator. Soak carrots and celery in water and store them in the refrigerator.
- Make 2 to 3 dozen whole grain muffins. Then freeze them.
- Make fresh fruit juice popsicles.
- Steam brown rice and store it in a sealed container in the refrigerator.

❖ Make a gallon of herbal iced tea sweetened with honey or birch sugar and store it in the refrigerator.

Fat Buster 5: EAT YOUR MEALS ON A SMALL PLATE

Because of my food addiction, I have trouble controlling the amount of food I eat, especially when I'm very hungry. Sometimes I love the taste of the food so much, I wish my stomach were bigger.

Overeating contributes to gaining weight even more than *what* we eat. By eating our meals on a smaller plate, we won't feel deprived or stuff ourselves.

Fat Buster 6: CLOSE DOWN SHOP THREE HOURS BEFORE BED

Many people don't realize how much overeating affects our body's ability to sleep. Even though we feel like sleeping when we stuff ourselves, our bodies have to work all night to digest the food. Therefore, overeating before bed prevents our body from doing restoration work while we sleep. When we go to bed on a fairly empty tummy, we'll sleep better and we'll wake more refreshed and without bloating.

Fat Buster 7: DON'T HAVE TOO MANY SWEET DREAMS

A word of caution about the "Sweet Dreams" chapter of this book. Those desserts were created as a healthy alternative to traditional, high-fat, high-calorie desserts. But too many carbohydrates, even natural sweeteners, can make us fat. I used to think if cookies were made with a healthy sweetener, then I could eat a dozen a day. But even the Bible says that too much honey is not good (Proverbs 25:27). Especially if you have a high-protein, low-carbohydrate body type, you shouldn't eat more than one healthy dessert a week, or you won't lose weight.

Fat Buster 8 : **STAY OUT OF THE POOL OF BLOATING**

I've spent most of my life swimming in a pool of bloating, or perhaps I should say, I felt as if a pool were swimming around inside of me. There have been times I felt so bloated, I'd swear you could hear my thighs swishing when I walked. If you couldn't, you could certainly hear my mouth moaning and groaning about my water retention. But I've finally found the ladder to lift me out of the puffy pool. Now that I have your attention, let's face some food facts together.

If your goal is to puff your eyes and dimple your thighs, then pour on that tasty salt, but if you're ready to deflate, then throw out that life killer and step into the healthy sea of salt. Sea salt is an excellent alternative and it does more than serve your salt cravings. It brings vital minerals to your body. In the "Shop with Me" chapter of this cookbook, you'll also find a buffet of beautiful seasonings, other than salt, that flavor your food without bloating your body.

Next…learn to bake without bloating. There's a little ingredient listed in many baked goods, particularly breads. I'm talking about yeast, which does more than bloat our baked goods. If you battle with bloating and/or exhaustion, remove the sugar and yeast from your daily diet and you should see dramatic results. When I was diagnosed with chronic fatigue syndrome, the doctor had me give up all foods containing yeast. Not only did I feel better, but by removing yeast from my diet, my bloating was gone and my cellulite started to disappear.

Think about what the yeast does to bread dough. It blows it up and puffs it out. Again, listen to the lifeguard of your body, and decide if you should give up yeast. Some of the other effects of yeast may be headaches, allergies, and fatigue. There are yeast-free breads and baked goods in health food stores along with a host of delicious, yeast-less recipes in the "Bake without Bloating" chapter.

Remember, we're not just talking about bloating. We're eating for excellence, so we can have the energy to swim through life like a champion!

Fat Buster 9 :   COOL IT

Cool your cravings for refreshing drinks by stocking up on sparkling mineral water and fruit juices from the health food store. Also, keep slices of oranges, lemons, and limes in Ziploc bags. Serve yourself a refreshing combination of mineral water, a splash of juice, and a squeeze of fresh lime, lemon, and/or orange in your drink. Serve it in a beautiful glass or goblet. This is an excellent alternative to soda or iced tea. Try different combinations of juices—be creative and have fun!

Fat Buster 10 :   HEALTHY SNACKS AT A PARTY

When you host a party or bring food or drinks to a friend's house, try something different from the usual greasy chips and sugary soft drinks. Here are some suggestions:

- fresh vegetable trays with low-fat dips
- fresh fruit trays with low-fat dips
- yellow or blue unsalted corn tortilla chips
- homemade salsas, such as pineapple, mango, or green chile
- popcorn (with low-fat butter flavoring)
- low-fat miniature muffins
- caffeine-free herbal teas (hot or cold)
- sparkling fruit punch bowl

To make the punch, blend sparkling mineral water, ice, and fruit juices (with no added sugar). Some good combinations are raspberry and pineapple, cranberry and apple, or cranberry and orange. It's a crowd-pleaser every time! And unlike soft drinks that rob the calcium and phosphorus from your bones, this delicious drink is good for you.

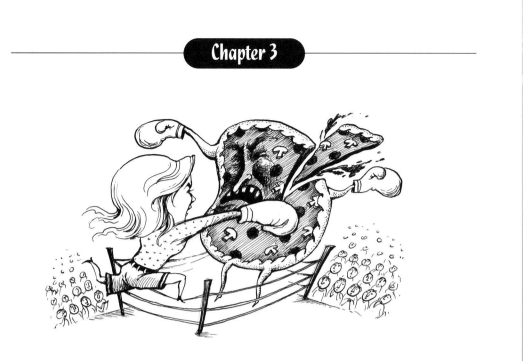

Chapter 3

Stop Fighting with Your Food

I spent years fighting with my food, and it all started when I began dieting.

I had been eating a high-protein, low-carbohydrate diet and feeling great. I had loads of energy, was losing weight, and was emotionally stable. As the saying goes, "If it's not broken, don't fix it." But being the curious individual that I am, I started reading up on all the latest diet information, which can be enormously confusing. Some diet plans said don't eat meat, others said eat all fruit, and others prescribed no fat and high carbohydrates. I drove my body nuts trying to follow the newest diet fads.

Why is it that some of us feel better eating one way and others thrive on an entirely different eating plan? And why do some of us gain weight on our tummies and arms and others on our rear ends and thighs? I've discovered that there is not one diet that works for everyone. But if you learn what diet works for you and follow it, you'll lose weight much more easily than you will if you eat the wrong foods for your body type.

In this chapter, we're going to discover what makes your body thrive and what makes your body burn out. Take a few moments to answer the following questions. Place a check mark by the statements that best describe your body and its reactions to food:

_____ **P** My body is shaped like an apple.
✓ **C** My body is shaped like a pear or hourglass.

✓ **P** I gain weight in my arms, back, and stomach.
_____ **C** I gain most of my weight in my hips and thighs.

Most of my excess fat is located in…

✓ **P** My arms and stomach
_____ **C** My thighs and hips

_____ **P** I crave sweets and breads constantly.
✓ **C** I crave rich, spicy, salty foods.

_____ **P** When I eat sugar, I feel tired within minutes.
✓ **C** When I eat sugar, I get an energy rush.

✓ **P** I lose weight faster eating chicken, salads, fish, and vegetables.
✓ **C** I lose weight faster eating whole grains, pasta, fresh fruit, and less fat.

✓ **P** I have to eat breakfast to start my day.
_____ **C** I prefer a light breakfast or none at all.

✓ **P** My blood sugar crashes when I wait too long to eat.
_____ **C** I can go hours without food if I have a caffeine fix.

How much sleep does your body require?

 P   6 hours when feeling well; 8 to 10 when tired

   C   8 to 10 hours for optimum energy

The time of your highest energy level is…

 P   In the morning, or following meals

   C   Late in the day

Do your hands and feet get cold at night?

   P   Often

   C   Sometimes in cold weather

When you're down, you're more apt to become…

 C   Depressed and tired

 C   Irritable and cranky

Total your: **P** scores _____6_____

                     C scores _____8_____

If you scored highest in the **Ps**, then we'll put you in the **Princess program.** Most likely your body is going to operate at optimum level on a high-protein, low-carbohydrate diet.

If you scored highest in the **Cs**, then we'll put you in the **Cherub program.** Most likely complex carbohydrates and low-fat foods will give your body its best performance.

I'm a Princess. When I eat too many complex carbohydrates, even healthy organic ones, I gain weight and get tired. On the other hand, my stepmother Susie is a Cherub. She gains energy by eating a combination of complex carbs, protein, and fruit. The following are the eating for excellence recommendations for both body types. It's important for you to pay attention to your lifeguard. You'll know within a week which plan is best for you.

♛ The Princess Plan

If you truly are a Princess type, your diet plan is high-protein, low-carbohydrates.

A Princess's breakfast

energy boost: First thing upon waking, before you eat, drink a large glass of water with a tablespoon of Barley Green Powder.

protein: hormone-free eggs, scrambled with veggies (any recipe in the "Egg in Your Face" chapter)

sweet tips: Because we princesses crave sweets so badly, I encourage you to drink mineral water with a small splash of juice and fresh lemons.

small serving of complex carbohydrates: 1 piece of yeast-free bread, or 2 Rye Crisps, or 1 small bowl of hot, whole-grain cereal (very little sweetener on cereal, preferably none)

A Princess's lunch

A princess should always eat raw veggies with protein—you'll feel great! So eat salad, salad, and salad with protein. Use as many different colors as possible (pick any recipe from "Veggin' Out on Daniel's Diet").

Note: Princesses can eat their favorite full-fat salad dressing and still lose weight. However, it's best to put your salad dressing on the side and dip. You'll save many fat grams by doing this and you won't make the Cherubs jealous.

A Princess's afternoon snack

<u>Afternoons are the hardest for us princesses</u>. Many times our blood sugar crashes and we want to artificially force our bodies to wake up, so we grab a caffeine-sugar fix. Don't do it! It's not worth the side effects of fat, depression, and exhaustion.

Choices:
- ♛ raw almonds
- ♛ low-sodium V-8 Juice

- "Cool It" drink
- hard-boiled egg
- a few bites of tuna salad
- sliced tomato with balsamic vinegar
- raw carrots

If you really want or need to finish your day strong, "go for the Green" again and drink Barley Green Powder in water.

A Princess's dinner

- protein of any kind: use the lamb, beef, fish, or meatless recipes in this book
- small portion of complex carbohydrates: brown rice, sweet potatoes, millet, or any whole grain
- any vegetable dish and any salad recipe

Diet data for Princesses

Eat *no* fruit while you're losing weight, little fruit while you're maintaining, and *no* caffeine or sugar. You may have one or two "Sweet Dreams" a week—not daily. Remember, if you're a Princess, sugar is a drug to you. It will kill your engine. Also, too much fruit or natural sugar will affect your energy level and weight loss.

Don't forget to drink lots of water throughout the day and don't let yourself get too hungry or too full. I've been able to keep my excess weight off for over seventeen years following this diet plan. If you're a Princess, I pray you'll be blessed by applying these principles to your daily eating habits.

The Cherub Plan

If you scored as a Cherub, then you're blessed; I've always envied Cherubs because I love carbohydrates.

A Cherub's breakfast

- fresh fruit of any kind
- whole grain cereal

- small portion of protein if desired
- Energy boost breakfast: fresh fruit smoothie blended with Barley Green Powder and crushed ice

Cherubs usually do much better on a very light breakfast.

A Cherub's lunch

Choose from the following foods:

- whole-grain sandwich with raw veggies and protein; fresh fruit
- any salad
- baked potato with veggies
- black beans and brown rice
- wrap sandwich (any recipe from "That's a Wrap!")

A Cherub's afternoon snack

I've noticed that most Cherubs don't snack on regular food; their weakness is usually eating empty calories of candy, caffeine, and soda. Don't do it! It will affect your weight loss and energy level, and keep you from experiencing optimum health. Your best snacks are raw veggies or raw fruit (don't combine them, but choose one). You can also eat something from the "Sweet Dreams" section of this cookbook—but eat it in moderation.

A Cherub's dinner

- a small portion of protein (hormone-free meat or vegetarian)
- complex carbs: potato, rice, whole grain pasta, beans, or lentils
- cooked veggies (see recipes in "Something's Cookin' in the Garden")

Diet data for Cherubs

Because your body thrives on complex carbohydrates, your type also does extremely well on a complete vegetarian diet (if the foods are combined properly to obtain enough protein).

Don't forget to drink lots of water throughout the day; you can also drink carrot juice or fresh-squeezed fruit juice once a day if you desire.

Make sure you keep your fat grams to a minimum, but don't go fat free. ✳
Don't eat diet foods or salad dressings full of chemicals.

Most importantly, enjoy the journey.

Chapter 4

Shop with Me

When shopping in a grocery store, don't get lost in the aisles of ill-
ness—instead, find your way to the hallways of health. The following is a list of spices, condiments, meats, proteins, sweeteners, nondairy products, whole grains, fruits, and vegetables
you'll need for the *Eating for Excellence* recipes in this book. There is also a
list of recommended food labels and vitamin lines. Most of the items can
be purchased at health food stores, gourmet stores, or in the health food
section of your local grocery store.

Spices, Herbs, and Seasonings

sea salt
black pepper
white pepper
cayenne pepper
oregano

Condiments and Dressings

Yoshida's Original Gourmet Sauce
plum sauce (Oriental)
low-sodium soy sauce
Cardini's Original Caesar dressing
honey mustard

cumin
rosemary
tarragon
turmeric
sage
garlic powder
fresh garlic
pumpkin pie spice
five-spice powder
curry powder
butter-flavored sprinkles
Molly McButter Buds
pure vanilla

✳ dijon mustard
✳ extra virgin olive oil
apple cider vinegar
rice vinegar
brown rice vinegar
red wine vinegar
toasted sesame seed oil
balsamic vinegar
Brian's poppy seed dressing
Colgin Hickory Liquid Smoke seasoning
low-sodium chicken broth
pepitas (toasted pumpkin seeds)

Sweeteners

birch sugar
honey: raw and organic; creamed, fruit-flavored
dark, unsulfured molasses
Sucanat (freeze-dried, raw cane juice)

Organic Meats and Proteins

hormone- and pesticide-free poultry, lamb, and beef (sold by D'Artagnan
Brae Beef
hormone-free eggs
organic tofu: silky, firm, and extra-firm
✳ fresh fish (not shark or catfish)

Whole Grains

barley flour
toasted oat bran
wild rice
brown rice
artichoke noodles

Organic Vegetables

potatoes
sweet potatoes
yams
tomatoes
carrots

brown rice cakes
  (unsalted, unsweetened)
rye flour
old-fashioned oats
polenta
unseasoned rye crisp
Wasa Crisp bread

celery
onions (green, red, yellow, and white)
fresh ginger
sugar snap peas
green beans
cabbage
salad greens (except iceberg lettuce)

Nondairy Products

Rice and Soy Products:
milk
sour cream
cream cheese
sliced cheese
ice cream

Organic Fruits

peaches
plums
apples
pineapple
melons (all kinds)
strawberries
raspberries

grapefruit
oranges
lemons
limes
bananas
blueberries

Healthy Food Labels

Health Valley
Alta Dena
Barbara's Bakery Items
Barbara's Dairy Free Products
Westbrae Natural Foods

Arrowhead Mills
Horizon Hormone-Free
Pamela's Cookies
Rice Dream
PAM nonstick spray (olive oil)

Vitamin and Nutrition Lines

Enzymatic Therapy
Aim Green Barley
Essentially Yours
Dr. Hagiwara's Green Magma

Body Wise
Amway
Ultimate Life
New Vision

Recipes

Chapter 5

Veggin' Out on Daniel's Diet

The following raw recipes are the key to renewed energy. Remember, live food makes you feel alive. Try to include raw veggies at lunch and dinner; your food will digest better and your body will be nourished. Remember: God blessed Daniel with extra strength, wisdom, and favor as a result of his diet and discipline.

Eating for Excellence Food Tip:

If possible, try to buy organic. Your vegetables will taste better and you will obtain the maximum nutritional benefits. If you can't find organic, buy the vegetable wash found in most grocery stores so you can wash away the pesticides sprayed on the crops.

COLD GREEK SALAD

SERVES 4 TO 6

3   cups shredded green cabbage

1   green bell pepper, julienned

1   cup English cucumber, julienned, peel on

3   medium tomatoes, wedged

1   cup sliced mushrooms

½   cup sliced black olives

⅓   cup crumbled feta cheese or freshly grated pecorino cheese

¼   cup extra virgin olive oil

   juice of 1 lemon

2 to 3   cloves garlic, minced

   sea salt and black pepper (or cayenne pepper) to taste

Toss all ingredients together in a beautiful large serving bowl and enjoy!

Note: You may use romaine lettuce in place of cabbage, but it will have to be eaten immediately, as it will not store well. Also, this can be a main dish with the addition of hormone-free diced cooked chicken breast or turkey, or a 6-ounce can of drained, flaked tuna.

MAKES ABOUT 1 CUP

GINGER HONEY DIP

This is a zesty topping for all kinds of fresh vegetables and salads.

¼   cup canola or safflower oil
¼   cup rice wine vinegar *(apple cider vinegar)*
1 ½   teaspoons finely grated fresh ginger
1   teaspoon Chinese hot mustard (optional)
4   tablespoons low-fat yogurt
2   teaspoons low-sodium soy sauce
2   tablespoons water
1   teaspoon toasted sesame seed oil
3   tablespoons raw or organic honey
1   clove fresh garlic, finely minced
     sea salt and white pepper to taste

Place all ingredients in blender or food processor. Pulse or blend until combined. Chill in refrigerator until ready to serve. This keeps well for several days in a covered container in the refrigerator.

Hot Italian Cabbage Salad

SERVES 6 TO 8

3	cups shredded green cabbage
3	cups shredded red cabbage
1	cup julienned raw carrots
1	cup chopped celery
½	cup chopped red bell pepper
½	cup chopped yellow pepper
½	cup chopped red onion
2 to 3	cloves garlic, minced
3	tablespoons extra virgin olive oil
1	teaspoon dried ground oregano (or 2 teaspoons fresh)
1 ½	tablespoons chopped fresh Italian parsley
1	teaspoon dried basil (or 2 teaspoons fresh)
½	cup low-fat crumbled feta cheese
	juice of 1 lemon
	sea salt and freshly ground pepper to taste

Place a large, nonstick skillet over high heat and generously coat with nonstick spray. Put first six ingredients in skillet. When vegetables just begin to wilt, add onion, garlic, olive oil, oregano, parsley, and basil. Cook two minutes more, then remove from the heat. Add the crumbled feta cheese and lemon juice and toss thoroughly. Season with salt and pepper if desired. Serve on beautiful plates and enjoy! (This is also good cold the next day.)

SERVES 6 TO 8   **HOT ORIENTAL CABBAGE SALAD**   **VEGGIES**

1 ½	cups green cabbage, coarsely chopped
1 ½	cups red cabbage, coarsely chopped
2	cups julienned carrots
½	cup julienned red bell pepper
½	cup julienned yellow bell pepper
2 to 3	cloves minced garlic
½	cup green onions, chopped
2	tablespoons extra virgin olive oil
1	teaspoon toasted sesame seed oil
4	tablespoons Yoshida's Original Gourmet Sauce or low-sodium soy sauce
⅓	teaspoon cayenne pepper (optional)

Place a large nonstick skillet over high heat and coat with butter-flavored nonstick spray. Add cabbage, carrots, and peppers to pan and stir-fry for 3 to 5 minutes. Stir in garlic, onions, and cayenne pepper; cook for 3 minutes. Remove pan from heat and add Yoshida's Gourmet Sauce or soy sauce, extra virgin olive oil, and toasted sesame seed oil. Stir thoroughly until completely coated. Serve with chicken, beef, fish, or brown rice, or serve alone. Enjoy!

VEGGIES

Low-Fat Potato Salad

SERVES 6 TO 8

This is a great accompaniment to barbecue, chicken, hamburgers, and hot dogs.

2 ½ to 3	pounds red potatoes (with skin on), cooked and diced (Add 1 ½ teaspoons sea salt to cooking water)
½	cup diced red onion
½	cup finely diced celery
¼	cup finely diced bread-and-butter pickles
¼	cup low-fat mayonnaise
1	cup nonfat plain yogurt
3	tablespoons raw honey
1 to 1 ½	teaspoons Liquid Smoke
2	tablespoons rice vinegar
2	tablespoons yellow or dijon mustard
1	teaspoon garlic powder or 1 minced garlic clove
	sea salt and freshly ground pepper to taste

Drain potatoes well and place in large mixing bowl. Add onion, celery, and pickles. In another small bowl, put mayonnaise, yogurt, honey, Liquid Smoke, rice vinegar, and mustard; mix well. Add garlic powder, sea salt, and pepper if desired. Blend thoroughly. Then pour over potato mixture. Fold until well blended.

Note: This keeps well in a covered dish in refrigerator for up to 3 days.

SERVES 4 TO 6   JAPANESE FUMI SALAD

This can be a substantial main dish with the addition of
1 ½ to 2 cups of shredded, cooked chicken breast.

4	cups shredded green cabbage
⅓	cup toasted slivered almonds (or blanched almonds)
2	tablespoons toasted sesame seeds
½	cup finely chopped green onions

Combine all ingredients in a large bowl.

In a small bowl combine all of the following except the fresh lemon or lime juice:

¼	cup canola oil
¼	cup rice wine vinegar
1 to 1 ½	tablespoons grated fresh ginger
1 ½	teaspoons toasted sesame seed oil
3	tablespoons raw honey
3	tablespoons low-sodium soy sauce
⅓	cup plum sauce
⅓ to ½	teaspoon white pepper
	fresh lemon or lime juice

Whisk together all ingredients thoroughly. Pour dressing over cabbage mixture and fold until well combined. Squeeze fresh lemon or lime juice over individual servings.

Note: Crispy chow mein noodles are a good addition—especially if you're feeding men and children.

ITALIAN SALAD PIZZA BREAD   SERVES 6

1	large prebaked whole-wheat pizza bread shell
¾	cup grated Romano cheese
3	tablespoons red wine vinegar
2	tablespoons fresh lemon juice
1	teaspoon raw honey
1	teaspoon sea salt
2	tablespoons water
1	minced garlic clove
½	teaspoon dried oregano (or 1 tablespoon fresh)
½	teaspoon dried basil (or 1 tablespoon fresh)
½	teaspoon freshly ground black pepper
½	teaspoon crushed red pepper flakes (optional)
¼	cup extra virgin olive oil
1	cup romaine lettuce, chopped
1	cup butter lettuce, chopped
2	cups chopped fresh tomatoes
1	cup chopped avocado
½	cup chopped green onions

Preheat oven to 400 degrees. Spray pizza bread shell with olive oil spray. Then lightly sprinkle Romano cheese on pizza bread. Place on cookie sheet and bake for 5 to 6 minutes, until slightly browned and cheese is melted. Mix together the next ten ingredients in a small bowl, then add olive oil and whisk thoroughly.

Mix together vegetables in a large bowl, toss with dressing, then put on pizza bread shell. Slice and enjoy!

SERVES 6 TO 8　　　　**CABBAGE PATCH VEGGIE MEDLEY**　　**VEGGIES**

(Or, The Case of the Disappearing Salad)

3	cups coarsely grated green cabbage
1	cup coarsely grated red cabbage
5	ears fresh uncooked corn, cut from the cob
½	cup chopped red bell pepper
½	cup sugar snap peas
⅓	cup chopped red onion (or green onion)
½	cup grated carrots
¼	cup roasted pepitas
½	cup low-fat mayonnaise
¼	cup rice wine vinegar
1	teaspoon dill weed
1 ½	teaspoons Liquid Smoke
¼	cup raw honey
1	teaspoon cumin powder
2	cloves garlic, minced
2	teaspoons poppy seeds
2	tablespoons chopped cilantro
½	teaspoon cayenne pepper
1	teaspoon sea salt
2	tablespoons spicy mustard (optional)
1	cup plain nonfat yogurt

Combine cabbage, corn, pepper, sugar snap peas, onions, carrots, and pepitas in a very large mixing bowl and set aside. In another bowl, combine mayonnaise, vinegar, dill, Liquid Smoke, honey, cumin, garlic, poppy seeds, cilantro, cayenne pepper, sea salt, mustard, and yogurt. Mix well, then pour over cabbage mixture. Blend thoroughly and serve. This salad keeps quite well—if there is any left!

Yam Salad

SERVES 4 TO 6

4   medium yams or sweet potatoes
1   cup pineapple chunks, drained
½   cup toasted slivered almonds
¼   cup pineapple juice
¼   cup low-fat mayonnaise
2   teaspoons apple cider vinegar
½   teaspoon garlic powder
1   teaspoon orange zest
2   tablespoons plain nonfat yogurt

Cook yams until tender yet firm. Peel and cut into 1-inch chunks. In a mixing bowl, gently combine all ingredients until thoroughly coated. Enjoy!

SERVES 6

CARROT SALAD

LOW-FAT/HIGH-FIBER

6 to 8 large carrots, well scrubbed and grated, but not peeled
   1 cup crushed pineapple, well drained (or use fresh pineapple)
   1 8-ounce container plain nonfat yogurt
   2 tablespoons low-fat mayonnaise
  ¼ teaspoon garlic powder
  ¼ teaspoon sea salt
  ½ cup raisins

Blend grated carrots and crushed pineapple in a mixing bowl. In another mixing bowl, combine yogurt, mayonnaise, garlic powder, and sea salt. Blend well. Add raisins and stir, then pour over carrots and pineapple and fold together.

Serve immediately or cover and chill in refrigerator until ready to use.

Note: ¼ cup pine nuts or 1 teaspoon orange zest are delightful additions.

ORIENTAL PEA SALAD

SERVES 4 TO 6 AS A SIDE DISH

1	16-ounce bag frozen peas, defrosted
½	cup diced roasted red pepper
¼	cup diced yellow onion
1	tablespoon toasted sesame seeds
1	tablespoon crunchy peanut butter
2	tablespoons nonfat mayonnaise
2	tablespoons rice wine vinegar
2	tablespoons raw honey
	sea salt and white pepper to taste

Pour peas into a large mixing bowl. Add red pepper and onion. Stir in sesame seeds, peanut butter, mayonnaise, rice wine vinegar, and honey. Add salt and pepper if desired.

SERVES 4 TO 6 **MEXICAN CORN SALAD**

This is a great side dish for a Tex-Mex dinner.

Toss the first six ingredients together in a large bowl:

1	16-ounce bag frozen corn, defrosted
¼	cup diced roasted red pepper
¼	cup diced green chiles
¼	cup thinly sliced green onions
2	hard-boiled eggs, coarsely chopped
½	teaspoon cumin (optional)
¼	cup nonfat or low-fat mayonnaise
2	tablespoons raw honey
½	teaspoon Liquid Smoke
2	teaspoons lime juice

Blend mayonnaise, honey, Liquid Smoke, and lime juice, then pour over the other ingredients and toss gently until well blended.

WALDORF SALAD

SERVES 4 TO 6

LOW-FAT/HIGH-FIBER

This is a low-fat version of the traditional salad. Granny Smiths or pippins are good choices for the green apples.

1	cup red or golden delicious apples, diced
1	cup green apples, diced
½	cup diced celery
⅛	cup dried chopped dates (optional)
¼	cup raisins
½	cup mandarin oranges, well drained
2	tablespoons sunflower seeds (dry-roasted or raw)
2	tablespoons slivered almonds or pine nuts
½	teaspoon sea salt
1	cup nonfat pineapple yogurt
2	tablespoons low-fat mayonnaise
⅓	cup pineapple juice

Combine the apples, celery, dates, raisins, mandarin oranges, sunflower seeds, and almonds in a large bowl. In a small bowl, whisk together the sea salt, yogurt, mayonnaise, and pineapple juice, then pour over the apple mixture and fold until all ingredients are covered with dressing. Chill in refrigerator in a covered container until ready to use.

Chapter 6

Something's Cookin' in the Garden

Cooked vegetables are great, especially for those people who are not used to eating much raw food. I love cooked vegetables especially in the winter. I think you'll enjoy the unique recipes we've provided for you—there's a buffet of flavors for your taste buds to enjoy.

 Eating for Excellence Food Tip:

Remember not to overcook your veggie dishes, especially when you stir-fry.

ZUCCHINI PANCAKES

SERVES 6 TO 8

GARDEN

4   medium zucchini, shredded and drained
3   medium red onions, chopped
1   clove garlic, minced
2   eggs, lightly beaten
½   teaspoon sea salt
¼   teaspoon cayenne pepper
⅓   cup feta or farmer's cheese, crumbled
2   tablespoons organic flour
½   teaspoon oregano
½   teaspoon basil

Combine the zucchini with onions, garlic, eggs, salt, pepper, cheese, flour, oregano, and basil. Mix well. Over medium-high heat prepare a non-stick skillet with nonstick butter-flavored spray. Drop zucchini mixture by one tablespoon at a time (this makes a small pancake). Cook about one minute, then turn over to brown on other side, about one minute. Serve immediately or freeze.

SERVES 6

LOW-FAT MASHED POTATOES

2 ½   pounds red or russet potatoes
        Molly McButter Buds to taste
        white or black fresh ground pepper to taste
        garlic powder to taste
        low-sodium chicken broth

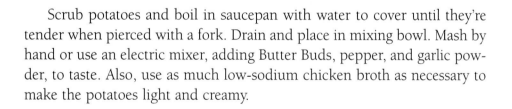

Scrub potatoes and boil in saucepan with water to cover until they're tender when pierced with a fork. Drain and place in mixing bowl. Mash by hand or use an electric mixer, adding Butter Buds, pepper, and garlic powder, to taste. Also, use as much low-sodium chicken broth as necessary to make the potatoes light and creamy.

POTATO PANCAKES

SERVES 6 TO 8

GARDEN

2 ½   pounds potatoes, peeled and grated
⅓   cup finely chopped onion
2   cloves garlic, minced
    sea salt and pepper to taste

Place grated potatoes in a strainer; rinse under cold water and let drain thoroughly before frying. Combine the potatoes with all other ingredients, and form the mixture into small patties (about 3 inches across). Heat a nonstick pan over medium heat and coat with nonstick butter-flavored canola or safflower oil. Brown patties on both sides and serve with breakfast, lunch, or dinner.

Note: Grated carrots and chopped red onion are nice additions and add gorgeous color to the potatoes.

WINTER SQUASH

1   butternut squash or
1   acorn squash or
1   spaghetti squash

Cut squash in half and place in a microwave-safe pan. Add 1 table-spoon water to the pan. Cover and cook for 12 to 15 minutes (because microwaves do not all cook the same, you may have to add more or less time), or until the squash is tender when pierced with a fork.

Seasoning the squash:

For butternut or acorn squash, add your choice of Butter Buds, honey, garlic powder, herb mixtures, 1 tablespoon olive oil, spaghetti sauce, low-fat Italian dressing, or cinnamon. Add sea salt and pepper to taste.

For spaghetti squash, scoop out the pulp onto a platter and add sautéed red, yellow, and green bell peppers, onions, and mushrooms. Sprinkle with a bit of rice parmesan cheese and sea salt and pepper to taste. You may add cubed, well-drained, extra-firm tofu to the sautéed mixture for a delicious, meatless low-fat meal.

COOKED RUTABAGAS OR TURNIPS

SERVES 2 TO 4

GARDEN

Root vegetables are delicious and healthy for you. However, many people don't eat them simply because they don't know how to prepare them. Try this recipe and see how easy they are to cook! Also try slicing raw turnips into julienne strips and adding to a green garden salad for a delicious crunch.

2 to 3 large rutabagas or turnips, peeled and cut into 1-inch cubes
    1 cup low-sodium chicken broth
    2 tablespoons Molly McButter Buds
    1 teaspoon garlic powder
      sea salt and freshly ground pepper to taste

Place rutabagas or turnips, chicken broth, Butter Buds, and garlic powder in a microwave-safe pan. Cover and cook 12–15 minutes, or until tender when pierced with a fork. Add salt and pepper to taste.

Serves 4 to 6 Squash Stir-Fry

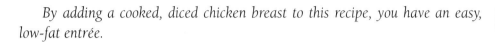

GARDEN

By adding a cooked, diced chicken breast to this recipe, you have an easy, low-fat entrée.

2   medium zucchini, sliced or julienned
2   medium crookneck squash, sliced
½   cup red bell pepper, julienned
¼   cup diced red onion
½   teaspoon dried Italian herbs (or 1 tablespoon fresh herbs of choice)
1   teaspoon Molly McButter Buds
1   clove garlic, minced
    sea salt and fresh ground pepper to taste

Prepare a skillet with nonstick spray (butter or garlic flavored) and place over medium-high heat. Place the zucchini, squash, red pepper, and onion in the pan and stir. Continue stirring for 3 to 5 minutes. Then add herbs and Butter Buds and stir for 2 to 3 minutes more. Add garlic, then turn off heat and stir everything until well blended. Season with salt and pepper if desired.

Remember: When you take the fat out you must add extra flavor, so you won't miss the fat and feel deprived.

GARDEN

STUFFED ZUCCHINI

SERVES 8 AS A SIDE DISH, 4 AS A MAIN DISH

Add extra-lean, seasoned ground beef to the filling of this dish for a satisfying main dish.

4   medium zucchini, cut lengthwise and with seeds scooped out
2   cups brown or wild rice, cooked and seasoned
3   cloves garlic, minced
⅓   cup red onion, diced
½   cup sliced mushrooms
3   cups low-fat, low-sodium marinara sauce
    Romano cheese (optional)

Preheat oven to 350 degrees. Combine cooked rice, garlic, and onion in a bowl and mix well. Spoon the mixture into the zucchini and place them in an oblong baking dish (make sure they sit upright so the rice mixture doesn't fall out). Mix the mushrooms into the marinara sauce, then pour 2 cups of the sauce (reserving one cup) over the zucchini. Cover with foil and bake in oven for 30 minutes, or until the zucchini are tender when pierced with a fork. Pour the remaining 1 cup sauce over zucchini. Remove and serve immediately. Sprinkle with freshly grated Romano cheese if desired.

SERVES 6 TO 8

COPPER PENNIES

6 to 8 scrubbed carrots, sliced
1 green bell pepper, julienned
1 red onion, sliced and separated into rings
1 can low-fat, low-sodium tomato soup
1 large garlic clove, minced
3 tablespoons apple cider vinegar
2 tablespoons extra virgin olive oil
2 tablespoons raw honey
   sea salt and pepper to taste
   cayenne pepper to taste

Place sliced carrots in a microwave-safe bowl and cook in microwave for 8 minutes. Remove from microwave and add green pepper and red onion; toss lightly. Return to microwave and cook 4 more minutes. Remove and cover with plastic wrap. Set aside.

In a large mixing bowl, combine tomato soup, garlic, vinegar, olive oil, and honey. Add salt and pepper to taste. Mix thoroughly and cook in microwave for 3 minutes on high, then combine with carrot mixture. Toss thoroughly, place in air-tight container, and chill for one hour or overnight. Serve.

HONEY-GLAZED COOKED CARROTS

SERVES 4 TO 6

GARDEN

6 large carrots, scrubbed and sliced
¼ cup raw honey
   sea salt and pepper to taste
2 teaspoons Molly McButter Buds
½ teaspoon garlic powder

Place carrots in microwave-safe bowl, cover bowl with plastic wrap, and cook for 9 to 10 minutes (until still firm to the bite).

Drain off any liquid. Then in a separate bowl combine the remaining ingredients. Add to carrots; toss until carrots are completely coated with mixture.

Note: ½ to 1 teaspoon orange zest adds terrific flavor.

SERVES 4 TO 5 — ITALIAN ASPARAGUS

1   pound asparagus
3   tablespoons extra virgin olive oil
6   large mushrooms, sliced
⅓   cup roasted red pepper, julienned
2   cloves garlic, minced
3   tablespoons red wine vinegar
1   tablespoon honey
     sea salt and pepper to taste

Blanch asparagus for 3 to 5 minutes, then drain. Place 1 tablespoon extra virgin olive oil in a small skillet and place over medium-high heat. Sauté mushrooms, red pepper, and garlic until just tender. Add to asparagus.

In a small bowl, combine 2 tablespoons extra virgin olive oil, 3 tablespoons red wine vinegar, and 1 teaspoon honey. Whisk together, then pour over asparagus mixture and toss thoroughly. Add sea salt and pepper to taste. Serve at room temperature or chill 1 hour before serving.

SWEET POTATO FRENCH FRIES   SERVES 4

GARDEN

4 to 6 medium sweet potatoes or yams, peeled and sliced into fries
garlic powder
sea salt

Preheat oven to 450 degrees. Spread out fries evenly on sheet pan or cookie sheet and spray lightly with butter-flavored oil. Sprinkle garlic powder and sea salt over fries.

Place pan in oven and cook until lightly brown, then turn them over with spatula and let brown on other side. Remove from oven and serve immediately.

Note: Low-sodium soy sauce, plum sauce, or toasted sesame seed oil can be used as a dipping sauce.

SERVES 4 LOW-FAT CLASSIC FRENCH FRIES

4 to 6 medium potatoes, peeled and sliced into fries
       garlic powder
       sea salt

Preheat oven to 450 degrees. Place fries in a strainer and rinse well, then drain and pat dry with paper towels (this makes the fries cook faster and get crispy).

Spread out fries evenly on sheet pan or cookie sheet and spray lightly with butter-flavored oil. Sprinkle garlic powder and sea salt over fries.

Place pan in oven and cook until lightly brown, then turn them over with spatula and let brown on other side. Remove from oven and serve immediately.

Note: Dried herbs of your choice are delicious additions; cayenne pepper gives them a kick.

Chapter 7

Bake without Bloating

We've already talked about the "bloatation" device called yeast. The following recipes are made with unbleached flour, natural sweeteners, and no yeast. As you begin to bake without bloating, you'll notice a dramatic difference in the way your body responds. Now when you eat baked goods, you'll be satisfying more than your taste buds. You will be giving your body the nutrition it needs from whole grains.

Attention Princesses: Go easy on the grain. It can turn us into pudgy Princesses if we eat too much. For extra protein, add some tofu to the muffin recipes. This will make them more moist and give you a boost of protein.

👍 **Eating for Excellence Food Tip:**

Don't mix raw fruit with grain; it causes indigestion.

APPLE OAT CRISP

SERVES 8 TO 10

BAKING

4   apples, peeled and diced

3   cups old-fashioned oats

1   teaspoon sea salt

3   hormone-free eggs, lightly beaten

1   cup plain soy milk or plain rice milk

2   teaspoons pure vanilla

⅓   cup organic honey

½   cup organic apple butter

2   teaspoons cinnamon

½   teaspoon nutmeg

Preheat oven to 350 degrees. In a large bowl, combine oats, salt, cinnamon, and nutmeg. In another bowl combine honey, apple butter, vanilla, milk, and eggs. Beat well, then pour the egg mixture into the bowl of oats. Mix well. Add diced apples, stir until combined. Pour mixture into a 9-by-13-inch nonstick pan. Bake for 35 to 45 minutes. Cool to room temperature and cut into 2-inch squares.

12 MUFFINS   PEANUT BUTTER AND PINEAPPLE MUFFINS WITH RAISINS

2	cups barley flour
1	cup oat bran
½	cup raw honey
2	teaspoon aluminum-free baking powder
2	cups crushed pineapple, undrained
⅓	cup crunchy peanut butter, melted
¼	cup raisins
3	hormone-free eggs
½	cup water or rice milk

Preheat oven to 325 degrees. Prepare a muffin pan with butter-flavored nonstick spray.

Combine all ingredients in a large mixing bowl and stir until just combined. Fill the cups two-thirds full. Bake for 20 to 25 minutes. Cool to room temperature and remove from pan.

Note: You can add fruit preserves as a topping.

LOW-FAT APPLE RAISIN MUFFINS

12 MUFFINS

BAKING

2	cups barley flour
½	cup oat bran
½	tablespoon aluminum-free baking powder
1	teaspoon baking soda
1	teaspoon sea salt
2 ½	teaspoons cinnamon
1	teaspoon nutmeg
½	cup raisins
½	cup rice milk
3	hormone-free eggs

Combine the above ingredients in a large mixing bowl, then add the following:

½	cup raw honey
2	cups peeled grated apples
2	teaspoons pure vanilla

Preheat oven to 325 degrees and spray a muffin pan with butter-flavored nonstick spray. The mixture will be lumpy. Fill muffin cups half full with the batter. Bake for 25 to 30 minutes. Cool to room temperature and remove from pan.

Note: If apples are waxed, peel them. If not, grate with skin on.

12 MUFFINS   LOW-FAT APPLE OATMEAL MUFFINS

2   cups barley flour
1   cup old-fashioned rolled oats
1   tablespoon aluminum-free baking powder
1   teaspoon sea salt
2 ½ teaspoons cinnamon
1   teaspoon nutmeg

Combine these ingredients in a large mixing bowl and then add the following:

1   cup rice milk
2   hormone-free eggs
1   teaspoon pure vanilla
¼   cup raw honey
¼   cup unsulfured molasses
½   cup apple juice (raw and unfiltered)
1   cup grated apples

Preheat oven to 325 degrees and spray a muffin pan with butter-flavored nonstick spray.

Mix all ingredients together until just combined. Fill muffin cups half full. Bake for 25 to 30 minutes. Cool to room temperature and remove from pan.

Note: If you make larger muffins, be sure to spray oil on the top of muffin pan, so muffins don't stick.

LOW-FAT ZUCCHINI MUFFINS   12 MUFFINS

½   cup oat bran
2   cups barley flour
1 ¾   teaspoons aluminum-free baking powder
1   teaspoon baking soda
1   teaspoon sea salt
2   teaspoons cinnamon
1   teaspoon nutmeg

Combine these ingredients in a large mixing bowl, then add the following:

⅔   cup rice milk
2   hormone-free eggs
⅓   cup raw honey
¾   cup strained prunes
1   teaspoon pure vanilla
1   cup grated unpeeled zucchini
1   tablespoon orange zest

Preheat oven to 325 degrees and spray a muffin pan with nonstick butter-flavored spray. Gently mix batter. It will be lumpy. Fill muffin cups half full. Bake 25 to 30 minutes. Cool to room temperature and remove from pan.

Note: You may substitute grated carrots for the zucchini.

12 MUFFINS

CRANBERRY ORANGE MUFFINS

LOW-FAT/HIGH-FIBER

½   cup oat bran
2   cups barley flour
2   teaspoons aluminum-free baking powder
1   teaspoon baking soda
1   teaspoon sea salt

Combine these ingredients in a large mixing bowl, then add the following:

1 ½   cups dried cranberries
2   teaspoons pure vanilla
2   hormone-free eggs
⅔   cup raw honey
½   cup orange juice concentrate
½   cup rice or soy milk
2   tablespoons orange zest

Preheat oven to 325 degrees and prepare muffin pan by coating it with butter-flavored nonstick spray.

Mix the batter gently. Fill the muffin cups half full. Bake for 25 to 30 minutes. Cool for 5 minutes, then remove from pan.

YUMMY YAM DELIGHT

This is a great side dish for poultry as well as a dessert.

BAKING

4	large yams
6	hormone-free eggs
½	cup raw honey
¼	cup rice milk
1 ½	teaspoons pure vanilla
½	teaspoon sea salt
2	tablespoons Molly McButter Buds
2	teaspoons cinnamon
½	teaspoon nutmeg

Preheat oven to 325 degrees. Wash yams and wrap each yam in plastic wrap, leaving a small opening for steam to vent. Bake in microwave 6 to 8 minutes on each side, or until tender.

When yams are done, scoop out the insides into a large bowl. Mash well and combine with eggs, honey, rice milk, vanilla, salt, cinnamon and nutmeg. Mix well, then pour into a 9-by-13-inch nonstick baking dish. Bake 45 minutes or until a toothpick inserted in the center comes out clean.

Serve with Butter Buds. Eat warm or chilled.

SERVES 8 TO 10   BROWN RICE CUSTARD TREAT

BAKING

COMPLEX CARBOHYDRATE, HIGH FIBER/HIGH PROTEIN

4	cups cooked brown rice
6	hormone-free eggs, lightly beaten
2	teaspoons pure vanilla
1	cup plain rice or soy milk
2	teaspoons cinnamon
1	teaspoon nutmeg
½	teaspoon sea salt
⅔	cup raw honey

Preheat oven to 325 degrees. Combine eggs, vanilla, milk, cinnamon, nutmeg, sea salt, and honey and mix well. Stir in rice. Pour the mixture into a 9-by-13-inch nonstick baking pan. Bake 35 to 40 minutes, or until a toothpick inserted into the center comes out clean. Cool to room temperature. Scoop into dessert dishes or cut into squares.

Note: You may add raisins if you wish.

BANANA TOFU OAT BRAN CAKE

SERVES 8 TO 10

BAKING

2	cups organic flour
2	cups oat bran, toasted
1 ½	cups well-drained, extra-firm tofu, mashed
⅔	cup pure maple syrup
2	hormone-free eggs
2	mashed ripe bananas
2	teaspoons aluminum-free baking powder
1	teaspoon sea salt
½	cup rice or soy milk
2	teaspoons pure vanilla
⅓	cup raisins
⅓	cup dried cranberries

Preheat oven to 350 degrees. Spray a nonstick bundt pan with butter-flavored nonstick spray. Combine flour, oat bran, tofu, maple syrup, eggs, bananas, baking powder, salt, milk, and vanilla in a large bowl. Mix well with a spoon. Add raisins and cranberries and stir until just combined. Pour into prepared pan. Bake for one hour or until a toothpick inserted into the center of the cake comes out clean.

PUMPKIN OATMEAL CAKE

SERVES 8

1	large can pumpkin
4 to 5	slices whole wheat bread, crumbled
1 ½	cups old-fashioned oats
3	hormone-free eggs
1	cup pure maple syrup or raw honey
4	teaspoons Oriental five-spice powder
2	teaspoons aluminum-free baking powder
1	teaspoon sea salt
1	cup rice or soy milk
2	teaspoons pure vanilla
½	cup raisins
⅓	cup raw shelled sunflower seeds

Preheat oven to 325 degrees. Spray a 9-by-13-inch nonstick baking pan with butter-flavored nonstick spray. Combine pumpkin, bread, oats, eggs, maple syrup, five-spice powder, baking powder, salt, milk, and vanilla in large mixing bowl. Mix well with a spoon. Add sunflower seeds and raisins and stir until just combined. Pour into prepared pan and bake for 75 to 90 minutes, or until a toothpick inserted into the center of the cake comes out clean.

ORIENTAL APPLE BREAD PUDDING

SERVES 6 TO 8

BAKING

4	cups cubed whole wheat bread
2	cups diced apples
1	cup rice milk
2	tablespoons melted butter
4	hormone-free eggs
⅓	cup honey
1	teaspoon pure vanilla
1 ½	teaspoons Oriental five-spice powder
1	teaspoon lemon zest
½	cup raisins

Preheat oven to 325 degrees. Spray a 9-by-13-inch glass baking dish with butter-flavored nonstick spray. Combine bread and apples in a large mixing bowl. Set aside. In another bowl, combine all other ingredients and whisk thoroughly. Pour this over the apple and bread mixture and mix until just combined. Pour the mixture into the prepared dish and bake for one hour. Serve warm or chilled.

SERVES 6 TO 8

MILLET AND EGG TREAT

- 2 cups cooked millet
- 6 hormone-free eggs
- 1 teaspoon sea salt
- 1 teaspoon pure vanilla
- ½ cup raw honey
- 2 teaspoons cinnamon
- ¾ teaspoon nutmeg
- ½ cup plain, low-fat rice or soy milk

Preheat oven to 325 degrees. Coat a 9-by-13-inch nonstick baking pan with butter-flavored nonstick spray. Set aside. Spray a skillet with butter-flavored nonstick spray. Place millet into hot skillet and cook until brown, stirring constantly. Set aside. In a large mixing bowl, combine eggs, salt, vanilla, honey, cinnamon, nutmeg, and milk. Mix well. Add browned millet to egg mixture and stir until combined. Pour into prepared pan and bake 45 to 60 minutes, or until a toothpick inserted into the center comes out clean. Cool to room temperature and cut into squares.

PUMPKIN TOFU TREAT

HIGH PROTEIN, COMPLEX CARBOHYDRATE

BAKING

1	1-pound, 13-ounce can pumpkin
2	cups extra-firm tofu, well drained and mashed
4	hormone-free eggs
1	teaspoon sea salt
2	teaspoons cinnamon
1	teaspoon nutmeg
1	teaspoon allspice
2	teaspoons pure vanilla
½	cup raw honey
3	tablespoons pure maple syrup
⅓	cup rice or soy milk

Preheat oven to 325 degrees. Prepare 9-by-13-inch nonstick baking pan with butter-flavored nonstick spray. In a large mixing bowl, combine pumpkin and tofu. Add remaining ingredients. Stir well with a spoon. Pour mixture into prepared pan and bake one hour, or until a toothpick inserted into the center comes out clean. Cool to room temperature, then cut into squares and serve.

Note: Organic vanilla frozen yogurt or rice or soy ice cream are terrific as toppings.

L. A. GRANOLA

This delicious, easy-to-make recipe is one of our family favorites.

3	cups old-fashioned oats
½	cup dry milk powder
½	cup whole wheat flakes
½	cup bran
1	teaspoon cinnamon
½	cup wheat germ
½	cup raw sunflower seeds
¾	cup raw almonds
⅓	cup sesame seeds
¾	cup raisins

Combine these ingredients, except raisins, in a large mixing bowl. In a saucepan over medium heat, combine the following:

¾	cup apple juice
⅓	cup honey
1	tablespoon pure vanilla
2	tablespoons unsalted butter

Preheat oven to 300 degrees. Pour the liquid mixture over the dry ingredients and mix until all dry ingredients are well coated. Spread mixture evenly onto a cookie sheet and bake for one hour, stirring occasionally. Cool to room temperature and stir in raisins. Store in refrigerator or freezer.

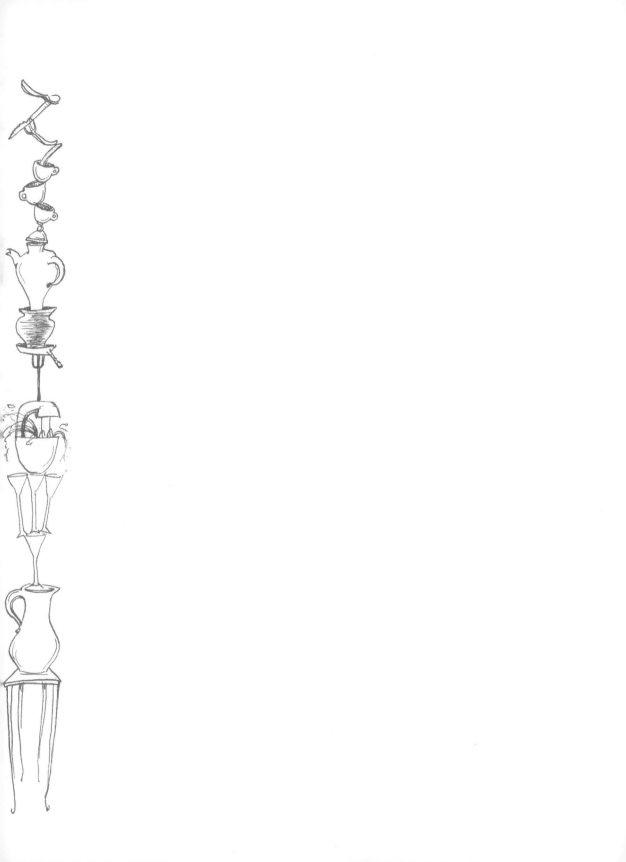

Chapter 8

Egg in Your Face

Okay, I know what you're thinking. Why are eggs in a healthy cookbook? Before you give up your eggs, face some facts. Eggs are the only food God created that contain all twenty-two amino acids. Next, eggs are loaded with lecithin, which helps our brain function properly. "What about cholesterol?" Good question. I'm not going to tell you that eggs don't contribute to high cholesterol, but I will tell you that years ago our ancestors on the farms ate eggs almost every day and they did not die of heart disease. The egg is not the problem; it's the processing of the egg that causes trouble.

👍 Eating for Excellence Food Tip:

Buy organic hormone-free eggs and enjoy the benefits and the great taste.

Egg Salad with Tuna

Serves 4 to 6

4	hard-boiled eggs, chopped finely
1	6-ounce can albacore or solid white tuna (packed in water)
⅓	cup finely chopped celery
⅓	cup finely chopped green onions
1 to 2	teaspoons poppy seeds
1	clove garlic, minced
⅓	cup low-fat mayonnaise blended with ½ teaspoon curry powder
⅓	cup nonfat yogurt
	juice of 1 lemon or lime
2 to 3	teaspoons raw honey
	sea salt and pepper to taste

In a medium mixing bowl, combine tuna with eggs and stir to combine. Add remaining ingredients. Mix all ingredients thoroughly and serve immediately or chill in covered container.

Serve on toasted whole wheat bread, brown rice cakes, or a garden salad.

EGGS

SERVES 6 TO 8

ITALIAN FRITTATA

8	hormone-free eggs
1 ½	cups diced zucchini
½	cup diced red onion
½	cup carrots, diced
½	cup red bell pepper, diced
1	teaspoon oregano
1	teaspoon basil
⅓	teaspoon cayenne pepper
2	tablespoons Molly McButter Buds
1	teaspoon sea salt
1 to 2	cloves garlic, minced
½	cup freshly grated Romano cheese

Combine eggs, oregano, basil, pepper, Butter Buds, and salt in mixing bowl and whisk thoroughly. Prepare a large nonstick skillet by spraying with butter-flavored nonstick spray. Over medium-high heat, stir-fry zucchini, onion, carrots, and red bell pepper. Add garlic when veggies are nearly cooked. Pour in egg mixture. Turn heat to low. Cover and cook slowly until egg mixture is solid. Then turn off heat and sprinkle cheese evenly over top. Replace cover and let stand for 5 minutes, then cut in wedges and serve.

Fresh Spinach Frittata

Serves 6 to 8

Eggs

8	hormone-free eggs
½	cup carrots, julienned
⅓	cup chopped red or green onions
⅓	cup chopped red bell pepper
3	cups fresh spinach
1 to 2	cloves minced garlic
1	teaspoon Liquid Smoke
2	tablespoons Butter Buds
½	teaspoon tarragon
½	teaspoon nutmeg
	sea salt and pepper to taste
½	cup freshly grated Romano or crumbled feta cheese

Combine eggs, garlic, Liquid Smoke, Butter Buds, tarragon, nutmeg, salt, and pepper in mixing bowl and whisk thoroughly. Set aside. Coat a nonstick skillet with butter-flavored nonstick spray and place over medium-high heat. Stir-fry carrots, onions, red bell pepper, and spinach until tender crisp. Add egg mixture. Turn down heat immediately and cover. Cook until the egg mixture is solid. Then sprinkle cheese evenly over the top. Cover and let cook 5 more minutes. Remove from heat. Let rest for 5 minutes, then cut into wedges and serve.

SERVES 6 TO 8

MEXICAN FRITTATA

8	hormone-free eggs
1	cup cooked brown or wild rice
1 to 2	cloves minced garlic
1	teaspoon cumin
1	teaspoon chili powder
⅓ to ½	teaspoon cayenne pepper
2	tablespoons tomato paste
½	cup yellow onion, chopped
½	cup green bell pepper, chopped
½	cup roasted red pepper, chopped
	sea salt to taste
2	tablespoons fresh chopped cilantro (optional)
¼	cup sliced black olives (optional)

EGGS

Combine eggs, rice, garlic, cumin, chili powder, cayenne pepper, and tomato paste in mixing bowl and whisk thoroughly. Set aside. Coat non-stick skillet with butter-flavored nonstick spray and place over medium-high heat. Stir-fry vegetables until tender crisp. Add egg mixture. Immediately turn heat to low and cover. Cook until egg mixture is solid. Top with cilantro and olives if desired. Remove from heat, let rest for 5 minutes, then cut into wedges. Season with sea salt to taste. Serve with fresh salsa and corn chips.

ORIENTAL SCRAMBLED EGGS

SERVES 4 TO 6

6 to 8   hormone-free eggs

1   clove minced garlic

3   teaspoons soy sauce

½ to 1   teaspoon toasted sesame seed oil

⅓ to ½   teaspoon white pepper

1   cup cooked brown or wild rice

1 ½   cups bean sprouts

½   cup chopped snow peas

½   cup chopped green onions

EGGS

Combine eggs, garlic, soy sauce, toasted sesame seed oil, and white pepper in a large bowl. Mix thoroughly and set aside. Coat skillet with butter-flavored nonstick spray and place over medium-high heat. Add rice, peas, and onions to skillet. Stir-fry 2 minutes, then add bean sprouts, and stir-fry 2 more minutes. Add egg mixture and continue to stir until eggs are firm, but not hard. Serve immediately with fresh pineapple, mango, and papaya on the side.

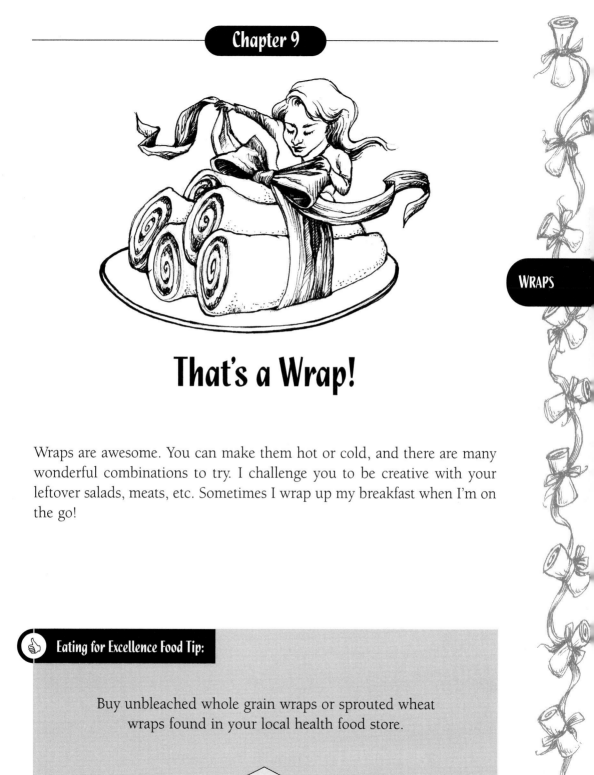

Chapter 9

That's a Wrap!

Wraps are awesome. You can make them hot or cold, and there are many wonderful combinations to try. I challenge you to be creative with your leftover salads, meats, etc. Sometimes I wrap up my breakfast when I'm on the go!

👍 Eating for Excellence Food Tip:

Buy unbleached whole grain wraps or sprouted wheat wraps found in your local health food store.

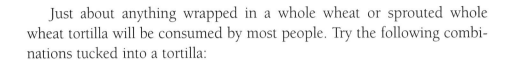

Just about anything wrapped in a whole wheat or sprouted whole wheat tortilla will be consumed by most people. Try the following combinations tucked into a tortilla:

Holiday Feast: smoked turkey breast, homemade cornbread stuffing, cranberry sauce, sliced onions, lettuce, and low-fat mayonnaise blended with poultry seasoning

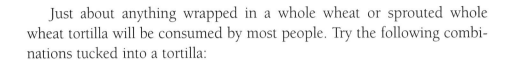

L.A. Combo: turkey breast, turkey bacon, green onions, lettuce or alfalfa sprouts, tomato, ranch dressing, and grated cheese (optional)

Honey, Eat Your Greens: smoked turkey breast, honey mustard dressing, ripe sliced olives, baby spinach, and rehydrated sun-dried tomatoes

Veggie Delight: smoked or roasted red pepper, olive and garlic hummus, lettuce, tomato, avocado, shredded carrots, green pepper, cucumbers, and low-fat creamy Caesar dressing

French Twister: grilled onions and mushrooms, sliced beef, grated Romano cheese or rice cheese, tomatoes, lettuce, and champagne or jalapeño mustard

Twice Hot Beef: warm sliced beef, jalapeño peppers, grated or sliced low-fat cheese (1 ounce), onions, tomatoes, lettuce, and Liquid Smoke blended with low-fat mayonnaise

Spicy Sloppy Salad: sliced chicken breast, spicy guacamole, lettuce, tomato, red onion slices, and combination low-fat bleu cheese and low-fat honey mustard

New Delhi: curried chicken salad (low-fat), pineapple, lettuce, alfalfa sprouts, and mango salsa or chutney

Tuna Boat: tuna pineapple salad (low-fat), avocado, lettuce, and honey mustard dressing

The Salmon Caper: smoked salmon, low-fat rice cream cheese, capers, cucumbers, red onions, lettuce, tomatoes, and low-fat mayonnaise blended with fresh dill

WRAPS

Chapter 10

Eat Your Beanies, Baby

Beans are an excellent source of protein and complex carbohydrates all in one. They are low in fat and loaded with nourishment, so eat your beanies, baby. I know that many people don't eat beans because of the side effects of gas. To avoid this, don't mix the beans with fruit (especially raw fruit).

Attention Cherubs: Bean dishes are excellent for your eating plan.

 Eating for Excellence Food Tip:

Wash your beans well before cooking them. If you have a problem digesting beans, there is a great product in your local health food store called Beano. It has enzymes that help the beans break down properly.

HARVEST SALAD

OR CORNIE BEANIE CABBAGE SALAD

1	large can of kidney beans, rinsed and drained
½	teaspoon curry powder
1 ½	cups frozen corn, defrosted, or fresh corn
½	cup grated carrots
⅓	cup chopped red onion
½	cup chopped celery
2 to 3	cloves garlic, minced
2	cups grated cabbage
	sea salt and pepper to taste
3	tablespoons low-fat mayonnaise
3	tablespoons honey mustard
3	tablespoons honey
	juice of 1 lime
1	teaspoon Liquid Smoke

BEANIES

Combine beans, curry powder, corn, carrots, onion, celery, garlic, cabbage, sea salt, and pepper in a large bowl. In a small bowl, blend mayonnaise, mustard, honey, lime juice, and Liquid Smoke. Pour over the vegetables, toss thoroughly, and refrigerate. Serve as a side dish or on a bed of romaine lettuce for a vegetarian entrée. Salad will keep in refrigerator covered for 3 to 4 days.

SERVES 6 TO 8   ASIAN BEAN SALAD

1	15-ounce can great northern beans, rinsed and drained
1	15-ounce can pinto beans, rinsed and drained
½	cup chopped cucumber, seeded
½	cup chopped celery
¼	cup chopped green onions
¼	cup chopped red bell pepper
1	tablespoon low-fat mayonnaise
1	tablespoon plain nonfat yogurt
1 ½	tablespoons ginger, freshly grated
1	tablespoon low-sodium soy sauce
3	teaspoons rice wine vinegar
1 ½	teaspoons fresh minced garlic
½	cup pineapple juice
2	tablespoons raw honey
1	teaspoon toasted sesame seed oil
½	teaspoon white pepper

BEANIES

Combine beans, cucumber, celery, onions, and bell pepper in a large mixing bowl. In another bowl, whisk together mayonnaise, yogurt, ginger, soy sauce, vinegar, garlic, pineapple juice, honey, toasted sesame seed oil, and white pepper. Pour dressing over vegetables and mix well. Refrigerate at least one hour. Serve on a plate of leaf or romaine lettuce.

GREEN BEAN SALAD WITH RED CABBAGE

SERVES 4 TO 6

2	cups grated red cabbage
2	cups blanched green beans (cooked 3 to 5 minutes in boiling water)
⅓	cup green onions
⅓	cup toasted slivered almonds or pine nuts (optional)
	juice of 1 lime
⅓	cup extra virgin olive oil
¼	cup balsamic vinegar or red wine vinegar
⅓	teaspoon cayenne pepper or white pepper
1	teaspoon sea salt
2	tablespoons honey
2	cloves garlic, minced

BEANIES

Combine cabbage, beans, onions, and almonds in a mixing bowl. Pour lime juice over the mixture. Toss thoroughly. In a smaller bowl, whisk together olive oil, vinegar, pepper, sea salt, honey, and garlic. Pour over vegetable mixture and toss. Serve immediately or chill, covered, for one hour. This will keep 2 days in the refrigerator in a covered container.

Note: Sautéed mushrooms are a nice addition to this salad.

SERVES 4

QUICK ITALIAN GREEN BEANS

HIGH FIBER

1   pound fresh or frozen green beans
1   roasted red pepper, julienned
1   garlic clove, minced
½ cup diced red onion
½ cup Italian vinaigrette dressing (or one of the dressings from this
     book)
   freshly ground pepper to taste

BEANIES

Blanch, steam, or microwave the beans until they are slightly tender. Place beans in cold water to stop the cooking process, then drain well. In a mixing bowl, combine beans with red pepper, garlic, and onions. Toss well. Add vinaigrette to the bean mixture and toss gently until well coated. Add pepper if desired. Serve immediately or chill for later use. In a covered container, this will keep in the refrigerator until the next day.

QUICK BAKED BEANS   SERVES 6 TO 8

HIGH FIBER/COMPLEX CARBOHYDRATE

2	large cans white or pinto beans, rinsed and drained
½	cup diced yellow onion
¼	cup raw honey or unsulfured dark molasses
3	tablespoons French's mustard
⅔	cup low-sodium organic catsup
1	teaspoon Liquid Smoke
1 to 2	cloves garlic, minced
1	tablespoon rice wine vinegar or balsamic vinegar
½	teaspoon freshly ground pepper

BEANIES

Preheat oven to 350 degrees. Place onions, honey, mustard, catsup, Liquid Smoke, garlic, vinegar, and pepper in small mixing bowl, blend well. Place beans in a 9-by-13-inch baking dish; pour dressing over and stir until combined. Set in oven and bake until hot and bubbly. Let rest for 5 minutes and serve.

SERVES 4   QUICK RED BEANS AND BROWN RICE

2	cups cooked brown rice, warm
4	cups red beans, rinsed and drained
1	teaspoon paprika
1 ½	teaspoons chili powder
½	teaspoon cayenne pepper (or to taste)
1 to 2	cloves garlic, minced
1	cup low-sodium chicken broth
1	teaspoon cumin
1	teaspoon Liquid Smoke
3	tablespoons tomato paste
	sea salt to taste
½	cup diced onion (garnish)

BEANIES

Combine beans, paprika, chili powder, cayenne, garlic, chicken broth, cumin, Liquid Smoke and tomato paste in large saucepan. Heat on high until just about to boil. Remove from heat. Put rice on plate and pour some beans on top. Season with sea salt to taste. Garnish with diced onion if desired.

BEANS AND CORNBREAD UPSIDE-DOWN CASSEROLE   SERVES 4 TO 6

3	cups kidney beans, rinsed and drained
1	15-ounce can salt-free crushed tomatoes
½	cup chopped green bell pepper
½	cup chopped onions
1	teaspoon sea salt
1	teaspoon oregano
1	teaspoon cumin
1	teaspoon basil
1 to 2	cloves garlic, minced
2	cups cooked brown or wild rice
1	tablespoon brown rice or balsamic vinegar
2	teaspoons raw honey
1	package organic cornbread mix

Preheat oven to 375 degrees. Coat a 9-by-13-inch glass baking dish with butter-flavored nonstick cooking spray. Combine all ingredients except cornbread mix in large mixing bowl. In a separate bowl, prepare organic cornbread batter according to directions on package. Spoon bean and rice mixture into prepared casserole dish. Then pour the cornbread mixture on top and bake until cornbread is golden brown, 20 to 25 minutes. Remove from oven, let rest 5 minutes, then cut into squares. Serve upside down (with cornbread on bottom) with a garden salad or mixed vegetables.

MAKES ABOUT 5 CUPS

LAYERED SMOKY REFRIED BEANS

1	15-ounce can low-sodium, fat-free refried beans
1	teaspoon Liquid Smoke
½	teaspoon cumin
1	clove garlic, minced
¼	teaspoon cayenne pepper
1 ½	cups plain nonfat yogurt
1 ½	cups fresh salsa
½	cup chopped green onions
1	cup sliced ripe olives

BEANIES

Combine beans, Liquid Smoke, cumin, garlic, and cayenne pepper. Mix well. On a beautiful plate or small platter, start layers: beans first, then yogurt, salsa, green onions, and olives.

Garnish with baked corn or pita chips, or served inside a sprouted whole wheat tortilla.

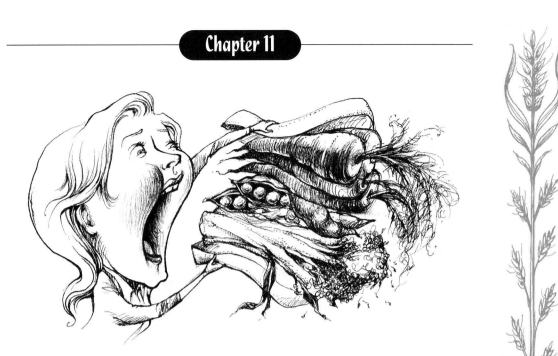

Chapter 11

Meatless Mouthfuls

The following pages are filled with recipes to replace meat dishes. If you're a full-blown vegetarian or just looking for a healthy, tasty alternative to the traditional American meat and potato diet, you and your body will enjoy the Meatless Mouthfuls.

Let's talk tofu: I know to some of you tofu sounds like a food for aliens, but the latest research proves the soybean to be an incredible benefit to our health. It's been proven to lower cholesterol and help prevent breast cancer.

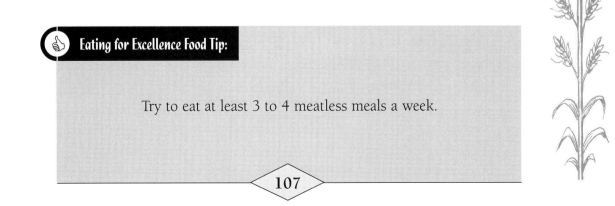

Eating for Excellence Food Tip:

Try to eat at least 3 to 4 meatless meals a week.

Tofu Cheese Pie

Serves 4 to 6

1 ½	cups L.A. Granola
1	teaspoon coriander
1	tablespoon raw honey
1	tablespoon flaxseed oil
1	tablespoon water
2	cups extra-firm tofu, mashed
1	tablespoon pure vanilla
¼	teaspoon sea salt
½	cup raw honey
2	tablespoons flaxseed or canola oil
1 to 2	tablespoons lemon juice
1	teaspoon lemon zest

Meatless

Preheat oven to 350 degrees. Mix together L.A. Granola, coriander, 1 tablespoon honey, 1 tablespoon flaxseed oil, and water. Press into 8- or 9-inch pie pan. In a medium mixing bowl, stir together tofu, vanilla, sea salt, ½ cup honey, 2 tablespoons flaxseed oil, lemon juice, and lemon zest. Add water if needed to make the mixture smooth and creamy. Pour into crust and bake for 20 to 25 minutes or until edges are lightly browned. Cool and serve with pure all-fruit jam or fresh fruit on top.

SERVES 6

STUFFED BELL PEPPERS

3	green bell peppers
3	red bell peppers
1	cup low-fat, small curd cottage cheese
1	cup chopped onion
2	medium tomatoes, diced
1 ½	cups cooked brown rice
1	clove garlic, minced
1	teaspoon oregano
1	teaspoon basil
1	teaspoon sea salt
½	teaspoon freshly ground black pepper
1 ½	cups tomato sauce (optional)

MEATLESS

Preheat oven to 350 degrees. Cut tops (save tops and chop the usable part for the filling) off peppers and clean out seeds; blanch in pot of boiling water for 5 minutes. Remove from water and drain. In a medium mixing bowl combine chopped pepper, cottage cheese, onion, tomatoes, rice, garlic, herbs, salt, and black pepper, and mix well. Stuff mixture into the bell peppers. Place peppers upright in a casserole dish that has been sprayed with nonstick spray. Pour tomato sauce over peppers if desired. Cover and bake for 30 to 40 minutes. Cool for 5 minutes and serve.

BASIC BROWN RICE   SERVES 4 TO 6

FAT FREE, HIGH FIBER, COMPLEX CARBOHYDRATES

Why brown rice or wild rice instead of white rice? White rice has been bleached, which removes most of the nutrients (minerals and vitamins), leaving only starch. Enriched white rice has vitamins added after the bleaching process. Brown or white—it's your choice!

4	cups filtered water
3	tablespoons low-sodium chicken bouillon
2	cups organic brown rice
1	tablespoon Molly McButter Buds
½	teaspoon curry powder, cumin, or turmeric

MEATLESS

Bring filtered water to a boil in a saucepan. Add all remaining ingredients. Stir well. When this comes to a boil, turn heat to low and cover. Let cook until all water is absorbed, 40 to 45 minutes.

Note: You may exchange 2 cups low-sodium chicken broth plus 2 cups filtered water in place of the bouillon and water.

Other nice additions include chopped green onions, walnuts, pine nuts, nutmeg, cayenne pepper, or oregano.

SERVES 4

BASIC WILD RICE

1 cup wild rice
1 ½ cups water
½ to 1 teaspoon sea salt
Molly McButter Buds to taste

MEATLESS

Place all ingredients in medium saucepan and cook over medium heat until mixture comes to a boil. Turn heat down to low and cook for 40 to 50 minutes, or until rice is tender and all liquid has been absorbed. Fluff with fork and serve.

Note: Low-sodium chicken broth can be substituted for the water.

THAI WILD RICE SALAD

SERVES 4 TO 6

3	cups cooked wild rice
1 ½	cups fresh sugar snap peas
1	cup chopped red bell pepper
1	tablespoon peanut butter
¼	cup low-sodium soy sauce
¼	cup low-sodium chicken broth
2	teaspoons fresh ginger, finely grated
⅓ to ½	teaspoon cayenne pepper
1	teaspoon garlic powder or 1 clove garlic, minced
3	tablespoons dry roasted peanuts
3	tablespoons fresh cilantro, finely chopped

MEATLESS

Combine rice, sugar snap peas, and bell pepper in a large mixing bowl. Set aside. In another bowl, combine peanut butter, soy sauce, chicken broth, ginger, cayenne pepper, and garlic powder, and mix until smooth. Pour sauce over rice mixture, and fold until all vegetables are well coated. Garnish with the dry roasted peanuts and cilantro.

SERVES 4 TO 6   EGGLESS TOFU SALAD

2	cups extra-firm tofu, well drained and mashed
½	cup celery, finely chopped
⅓	cup red or green onion, chopped finely
⅓	cup slivered toasted almonds or toasted sunflower seeds
¼	cup nonfat plain yogurt
¼	cup low-fat mayonnaise
2	tablespoons lemon or lime juice
2	tablespoons honey mustard
1	teaspoon curry powder or cumin
1	teaspoon garlic powder or 1 clove garlic, minced
¼	teaspoon white pepper
½	teaspoon dill weed
¾	teaspoon Liquid Smoke (optional)

MEATLESS

Combine all ingredients in mixing bowl and fold until well mixed. Serve immediately or refrigerate until needed.

Use as a filling with whole wheat pitas or any organic whole grain bread, or serve on top of a luscious green salad.

TOFU SUB SANDWICHES

SERVES 4 TO 6

1   pound extra-firm tofu
    soy or tamari sauce
    toasted almond meal
    onion powder
    garlic powder
    whole wheat rolls
    onions
    tomatoes
    bell peppers

MEATLESS

   Cut tofu into 1/4-inch slices. Marinate in soy or tamari sauce for 20 to 30 minutes. Drain tofu and dust with toasted almond meal, then sprinkle with onion and garlic powders. Coat a nonstick skillet with cooking spray, and brown tofu over medium-high heat. Place on whole wheat rolls and top with sautéed or raw onions, tomatoes, and bell peppers. Enjoy!

Serves 4 to 6   Hummus with Roasted Red Pepper Garlic

Complex Carbohydrate, High Fiber

2 cups cooked garbanzo beans, drain and reserve liquid
1 teaspoon ground cumin
⅓ cup nonfat or low-fat yogurt
½ cup chopped roasted red pepper
1 garlic clove, minced
  sea salt and cayenne pepper to taste
½ teaspoon Liquid Smoke
1 teaspoon lemon juice
1 teaspoon finely chopped chives or green onions

Place all ingredients in a blender or food processor, with the yogurt on the bottom. Puree until smooth. You may use the reserved garbanzo bean liquid if you want a thinner puree. Adjust seasoning to taste. Chill in refrigerator at least 24 hours to let the beans absorb the lemon so that the mixture is less acidic. Serve with whole wheat pita chips, brown rice cakes, or whole grain breads.

Note: Fresh basil, sun-dried tomatoes, black olives, curry powder, red onions, pesto, or toasted sesame seed oil are terrific additions. Be creative!

SWEET HUMMUS   SERVES 4 TO 6

2	cups cooked garbanzo beans, well drained
½	cup nonfat plain yogurt
1 ½	teaspoons pure vanilla
⅓	cup raw honey
1	teaspoon cinnamon
1	tablespoon tahini or almond butter

MEATLESS

Place all ingredients in a blender or food processor, with the yogurt on the bottom. Puree until smooth. If you want the mixture thicker, use less yogurt. If you like it thinner, add more yogurt. Serve on whole grain toast, brown rice cakes, or baked whole wheat tortilla wedges.

SERVES 3 TO 4

HOT SPINACH SALAD

MEATLESS

6	cups cleaned spinach
2 to 3	cloves garlic, minced
2	tablespoons extra virgin olive oil
	sea salt and pepper to taste

Heat a large nonstick skillet on high and coat with butter-flavored non-stick spray. Place spinach in skillet, stirring constantly. When slightly wilted, add garlic and the olive oil. Cook 1 ½ minutes, stirring constantly, and add salt and pepper to taste. Remove from heat. Let rest for 1 minute and then serve.

Option: During the last 30 seconds of cooking, add 1 cup drained, extra-firm tofu cut in 1-inch chunks.

Some delicious toppings are crispy turkey bacon bits, a splash of balsamic vinegar, or a drizzle of toasted sesame seed oil.

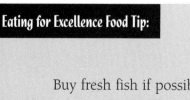

Chapter 12

Somethin's Fishy

During biblical times, people ate fish regularly. Many of us don't cook fish because we don't know how to prepare it so that it tastes good. If you're ready to dive into the water world of fish, I'm sure you'll enjoy the following quick, easy, tasty fish recipes. Keep in mind that most fish is low in fat and loaded with vitamin A and essential oils.

👍 **Eating for Excellence Food Tip:**

Buy fresh fish if possible and cook it the same day.

HEY, SHRIMP, RICE TO KNOW YOU!

SERVES 4

(SHRIMP AND RICE SALAD)

1	pound medium cooked shrimp
1	cup cooked brown or wild rice
½	cup chopped green onions
½	cup sliced water chestnuts or julienned jicama
2	medium tomatoes, cut into wedges
2	cups romaine lettuce, torn or chopped
2	cups butter lettuce, torn
	juice of 1 lime (incorporate some pulp)
1	garlic clove, minced
½	teaspoon sea salt
½	teaspoon cumin
½	teaspoon white pepper
3	tablespoons rice vinegar
1	tablespoon water
1 ½	tablespoons raw honey
¼	cup extra virgin olive oil

FISH

Combine shrimp, rice, onions, and water chestnuts. Arrange lettuce and tomatoes on 4 salad plates, then portion the shrimp mixture onto each plate. In a small bowl, whisk together lime juice, garlic, sea salt, cumin, white pepper, vinegar, water, and honey; then add olive oil and whisk well again. Drizzle dressing over shrimp and serve.

SPINACH BOW TIE PASTA WITH TUNA

SERVES 4 TO 6

1   6-ounce can solid water-packed white or albacore tuna, drained
3   cups cooked spinach bow tie pasta
½   cup frozen peas, thawed
½   cup chopped celery
⅓   cup chopped red onion
⅓   cup chopped yellow, green, or red bell pepper
½   cup cherry tomatoes, halved
1   teaspoon sea salt
3   tablespoons low-fat mayonnaise
4   tablespoons red wine vinegar
1   tablespoon dried tarragon (or 2 tablespoons fresh)
1   clove garlic, minced
2   tablespoons water
¼   cup extra virgin olive oil
1   tablespoon raw honey
2   tablespoons fresh lime juice
    slivered toasted almonds for garnish

FISH

Combine tuna, pasta, peas, celery, red onion, bell pepper, and cherry tomatoes in large bowl. In a small bowl, whisk together sea salt, mayonnaise, vinegar, tarragon, garlic, water, olive oil, honey, and lime juice. Pour over tuna mixture and toss thoroughly. Serve on a bed of leaf or bibb lettuce and garnish with slivered toasted almonds.

FISH FILLETS WITH LEMON BUTTER & GARLIC   SERVES 2

2   medium fish fillets
2   tablespoons Molly McButter Buds
1   teaspoon garlic powder
    freshly ground pepper to taste
    juice of 1 lemon

FISH

Place fish fillets on microwave-safe plate. In a small bowl, combine Butter Buds and garlic powder. Blend well. Add fresh ground pepper to taste. Squeeze the juice from 1 lemon on both sides of the fillets, then sprinkle the butter-garlic mixture on both sides of the fillets.

Cover and bake in microwave on high until the fish is opaque and flakes easily with a fork, about 5 to 7 minutes. It isn't necessary to turn over the fillets unless they are very thick.

Note: Basil, tarragon, or dill is a nice addition to the butter-garlic mixture.

The fish is also delicious steamed, broiled, or grilled. Do not overcook the fish (it's tough and dry when overdone).

FISH MARINADES

The following are a marinade and an herb/spice dry rub that can be put on your fish before cooking. They add delicious flavor and no fat.

Oriental Marinade

¼   cup Yoshida Gourmet sauce or 1/4 cup low-sodium soy sauce
¼   cup plum sauce
2   cloves garlic, minced
     juice of 1 lime
½   tablespoon minced fresh ginger

Mix thoroughly, then pour over 2 medium fish fillets in a dish with cover or a Ziploc bag. Refrigerate at least 1 hour, preferably longer. Serve with brown or wild rice. Squeeze fresh lemon or lime over fish before eating.

FISH

Hot and Spicy Dry Rub

½   teaspoon paprika
½   teaspoon sea salt
1   teaspoon minced parsley
1   teaspoon garlic powder
1   teaspoon lemon pepper
½   teaspoon dill

Mix all ingredients together in a small bowl. Rub generously over 2 medium moist fish fillets. Refrigerate until needed, or cook immediately.

French Glazed Fish

- 1 pound fish fillets (red snapper, sole, or orange roughy)
- ¼ cup low-fat french dressing
- 2 tablespoons all-fruit apricot jam
- 3 tablespoons all-fruit orange pineapple jam
- 2 tablespoons dried onion
- 2 tablespoons water
- ¼ teaspoon white pepper

FISH

Preheat oven to broil. Combine all ingredients except fish in a small bowl. Heat in microwave just until jam is melted, then stir well.

Place fillets on nonstick baking pan coated with butter-flavored non-stick spray. Broil 3 to 5 minutes, or until fish flakes easily with a fork. Pour sauce over the fish and serve immediately. Fresh carrots and french-cut green beans are nice accompaniments to the fish.

SERVES 4

LEMON DILL FISH

1	pound fish fillets (red snapper, sole, or orange roughy)
¼	cup low-sodium chicken broth
4 to 6	slices lemon
1	teaspoon Molly McButter Buds
½	teaspoon white pepper
1	teaspoon dried parsley
½	teaspoon dried dill (or 1 teaspoon minced fresh dill)

FISH

Preheat oven to broil. Arrange lemon slices on a nonstick baking pan and place the fish on top of them. Pour chicken broth over fish. Sprinkle Butter Buds, pepper, parsley, and dill over fish. Broil 8 to 10 minutes, or until fish is opaque. Serve with spinach salad and brown rice pilaf.

Chapter 13

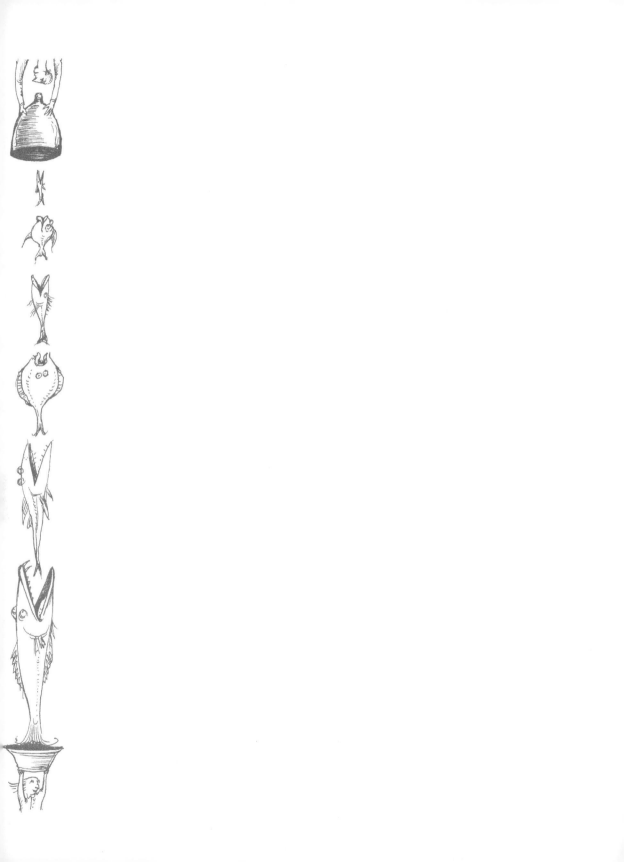

Shazam! It's Lamb

Lamb is an excellent source of protein. Its unique flavor gives variety to your meals. Here is a variety of ways to cook your lamb. I hope you'll get adventurous and try them.

LAMB

Eating for Excellence Food Tip:

Any meat is best eaten the same day. If you do keep it for leftovers, put it in the refrigerator immediately after serving it. Even if it's still warm, this will avoid the risk of food poisoning.

HEART-HEALTHY SPANISH RICE   SERVES 4 TO 6

1	pound ground lamb, browned and well drained
2	cups cooked brown rice
½	cup chopped red bell pepper
½	cup chopped green bell pepper
½	cup chopped onion
1 ½	cups chopped tomatoes
2	teaspoons raw honey
1	teaspoon garlic powder
1	teaspoon sea salt
2	teaspoons chili powder (or more if you like spicy)
¼ to ⅓	teaspoon cayenne pepper (optional)
1	teaspoon paprika
½	teaspoon cumin

LAMB

Combine lamb and cooked brown rice in a large skillet. In another skillet, stir-fry peppers and onions over medium-high heat. Add peppers, onions, tomatoes, honey, and spices to the skillet with the rice and lamb. Mix well, cover, and simmer for 5 minutes. Serve as an entrée for a Mexican meal or tucked into a tortilla for a quick lunch.

SERVES 4 TO 6

LAMB KABOBS

2 to 3 pounds lean lamb, cut in 1-inch cubes
   1 red onion, cut in 1-inch cubes
   1 green bell pepper, cut in 1-inch cubes
   1 yellow bell pepper, cut in 1-inch cubes
   1 cup pineapple juice
  ¼ cup low-sodium soy sauce
  2 teaspoons minced garlic
  2 tablespoons orange juice concentrate
  ⅓ teaspoon white pepper

LAMB

Soak wooden skewers in water about 30 minutes before use to prevent buckling or burning. Assemble lamb, onion, and peppers on skewers, alternating meat and vegetables. Place in a large pan or Ziploc bag. In a small bowl mix pineapple juice, soy sauce, garlic, orange juice concentrate, and white pepper. Pour marinade over kabobs. Cover pan or close bag, and place in the refrigerator for at least one hour, turning kabobs periodically.

Cook kabobs on the grill or in the broiler and brown on all sides. Serve with brown or wild rice pilaf.

SUCCULENT GROUND LAMB PATTIES

MAKES 5 TO 6 PATTIES

2   pounds ground lamb
1   teaspoon lemon zest
2   teaspoons dehydrated onion
1   clove garlic, minced
2   hormone-free eggs
1   teaspoon dried parsley (or 1 tablespoon fresh)
1   teaspoon sea salt
½ to 1 teaspoon freshly ground black pepper
6 to 8 whole wheat crackers, crushed
    ½   teaspoon ground rosemary or nutmeg or tarragon (optional)

LAMB

Preheat broiler or grill. Combine all ingredients in a large mixing bowl and stir well. Form into patties; place patties in broiler or on grill. Cook until browned on both sides and serve on whole grain buns with your favorite low-fat condiments.

SERVES 4 TO 6   LAMB PITAS

2	pounds lean ground lamb
1	teaspoon lemon pepper
½ to 1	teaspoon sea salt
2	teaspoons dehydrated onion
1	teaspoon garlic powder or 1 clove garlic, minced
2	teaspoons chopped fresh parsley
½	teaspoon ground rosemary
1	teaspoon minced fresh mint
4 to 6	whole wheat pitas, warmed

LAMB

Coat a large nonstick skillet with cooking spray and place over medium-high heat. Add all ingredients except pitas and cook the lamb until browned. Fill pitas with lamb mixture. Serve with fresh chopped lettuce or alfalfa sprouts.

Note: A cucumber dressing is a great finishing touch. Simply mix 1 cup low-fat rice sour cream or yogurt with ½ cup crushed seeded cucumber and ½ teaspoon dill weed. Stir well and drizzle over lamb.

European Style Ground Lamb and Rice   Serves 6 to 8

2   pounds ground lamb
3   cups cooked brown rice*
½ to 1 teaspoon sea salt
½   teaspoon onion powder
1   teaspoon garlic powder or 1 clove garlic, minced
1   teaspoon five-spice powder
⅓   teaspoon white pepper
    romaine or butter lettuce
    green onions and pine nuts (garnish)

LAMB

Brown lamb in a large nonstick skillet with sea salt, onion powder, garlic, five-spice powder, and white pepper. Stir together browned lamb and rice in a mixing bowl. Garnish a large plate or platter with romaine or butter lettuce leaves. Mound lamb and rice mixture in center. Garnish with chopped green onions and pine nuts. (Another option is to roll up mixture in individual lettuce leaves.) Serve with toasted pita bread.

* Cook rice with 2 teaspoons Butter Buds, 3 teaspoons fresh chopped parsley, and ½ teaspoon lemon zest.

SERVES 6 TO 8

LEG OF LAMB

5- to 6- pound leg of lamb
juice of 2 lemons
3 to 6 cloves garlic, minced
2 teaspoons sea salt
2 teaspoons dried rosemary, crushed
1 ½ teaspoons freshly ground pepper
4 to 6 bay leaves

LAMB

Preheat oven to 350 degrees. Trim all visible fat from lamb and put it into a roasting pan. Brush lemon juice over meat. Combine garlic, salt, rosemary, and pepper, and sprinkle over entire leg of lamb. Place bay leaves around lamb in pan. Cover pan completely with foil and place in oven. Cook for one hour, then remove meat from oven, discard foil, and return meat to oven to cook for 30 to 45 minutes more. Turn meat over halfway through cooking time. Cook the meat until it's barely pink and juicy. Take lamb from oven, let rest for 10 minutes, then slice and serve with mint jelly.

Note: You may make slits in the meat and insert whole garlic cloves in place of the minced garlic.

What's Your Beef?

Beef—what is beef doing in this cookbook? Believe me, I prayed long and hard about using any animal products in this book. But, after much study of God's Word, I found that even before Noah, God's people ate meat. God instructed Noah to bring animals on the boat in twos so they could reproduce after the flood. He also instructed them to bring animals to eat, and Jews ate the meat from the burnt offerings. However, I eat very little red meat—and when I do it's hormone-free beef. If you eat beef, go easy but enjoy!

There are a few poultry recipes in this chapter as well. I almost never eat chicken because of the way it's processed. Many people get very ill each year as a result of salmonella poisoning. In fact, 70 percent of all food poisoning deaths have been connected to chicken. However, hormone-free skinless chicken breasts can be very nutritious and are delicious in these dishes.

BEEF

ROAST BEEF

4- to 6-pound very lean beef roast

    4   tablespoons dehydrated onion

    2   teaspoons sea salt

1 to 2 teaspoons garlic powder or 2 to 3 cloves garlic, minced
        freshly ground black pepper to taste

    6   bay leaves

BEEF

Preheat oven to 350 degrees. Spray a large cast-iron skillet or Dutch oven with butter-flavored nonstick spray and place over medium-high heat. Sprinkle the beef on both sides with the dehydrated onion, sea salt, garlic powder, and black pepper. (If using fresh garlic, do not add to beef until it's in the roasting pan.) Sear the meat on both sides until well browned. Remove from pan and place in a metal or glass roasting pan. Add bay leaves, 3 on each side. Cover meat with aluminum foil and put into oven to bake for 1 ½ to 2 hours, depending on how well done you like your beef. If you are making pot roast, turn the meat over after one hour, remove foil, and add potatoes, carrots, celery, and onions to roasting pan. Return pan to oven for another 45 to 60 minutes. Remove from oven and let rest for 10 minutes before slicing.

SERVES 4   TURKEY WALDORF SALAD WITH SMOKY DRESSING

1	red apple, diced
1	yellow apple, diced
½	cup chopped celery
½	pound cubed cooked hormone-free turkey or chicken breast
¼	cup toasted chopped walnuts
	juice of 1 lime
4	tablespoons low-fat mayonnaise
¼	cup plain nonfat yogurt
½	teaspoon lemon zest
2	tablespoons raw honey
3	teaspoons apple cider vinegar
1	teaspoon Liquid Smoke
½	teaspoon sea salt
1	teaspoon curry powder
2	tablespoons water
⅓	cup pineapple juice

BEEF

In a large mixing bowl, combine the first 5 ingredients. Squeeze lime juice over all and mix thoroughly, then refrigerate one hour or until thoroughly chilled. In a small mixing bowl, combine remaining ingredients and whisk thoroughly. Chill in refrigerator, then pour over apple/turkey mixture. Mix until well blended and serve on butter lettuce leaves.

QUICK CREAMY CHICKEN STIR-FRY   SERVES 6

6	hormone-free boneless, skinless chicken breasts, cut into 1-inch pieces
1	teaspoon garlic powder
½	teaspoon freshly ground black pepper
1 ¼	cup low-fat ranch dressing
2	tablespoons fresh lime juice
2	tablespoons raw honey

BEEF

Coat a large nonstick skillet with butter-flavored nonstick spray and place over medium-high heat. Add chicken to pan and brown lightly, then add garlic powder and pepper and finish browning chicken. Turn down heat to low and add ranch dressing, lime juice, and honey. Toss until meat is well coated, then serve immediately with mashed potatoes, oven-baked french fries, or brown rice, and a salad of mixed greens.

SERVES 6 TO 8

HOT ORIENTAL CHICKEN SALAD

3   cups shredded green cabbage
3   cups shredded red cabbage
1   cup julienned carrots
1   cup julienned celery
2   cups diced cooked chicken breast, skinless and hormone-free
½   cup chopped green onions
2   cloves garlic, minced
    white pepper to taste
½   cup plum sauce
⅓   cup Yoshida's Original Gourmet Sauce
2   teaspoons toasted sesame seed oil
¼   cup rice wine vinegar
    chopped green onions (garnish)

Coat a large nonstick skillet or wok with butter-flavored nonstick spray and place over high heat. Place cabbage, carrots, and celery into pan and stir-fry until vegetables just begin to wilt. Turn heat to low. Add chicken, onions, garlic, and white pepper, and cook for 2 more minutes. Add plum sauce, Yoshida's Gourmet Sauce, toasted sesame seed oil, and vinegar, then remove from heat. Stir until well combined and serve immediately. Garnish with green onions.

Note: Toasted sunflower kernels or slivered toasted almonds are good toppings.

BEEF

French Glazed Chicken

SERVES 2 TO 4

1   pound boneless, skinless chicken breast or thighs cut into bite-size
       pieces

¼   cup low-fat french dressing

2   tablespoons all-fruit apricot jam

3   tablespoons all-fruit orange-pineapple jam

2   tablespoons dried onion

2   tablespoons water

¼   teaspoon white pepper

BEEF

Preheat broiler. Broil chicken for 8 to 10 minutes until opaque but not dry. Let rest. In a small microwave-safe bowl, stir together all remaining ingredients. Heat in microwave just until jam is melted. Toss chicken until all pieces are well coated. Serve immediately.

Chapter 15

You Crock Me Up

If you don't own a Crock-Pot, get one. They're awesome. You can prepare dinner in the morning, let it cook all day, and not have to worry about it burning your house down while you're gone. For accident-prone people like me, this is a great way to cook. So crock yourself up and enjoy the following recipes.

CROCK POT

👍 **Eating for Excellence Food Tip:**

If you get a big enough Crock-Pot, you can soak your feet in it!

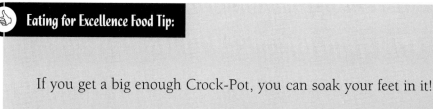

RASPBERRY DRUMSTICKS

SERVES 5

5   skinless drumsticks with thighs attached
3   tablespoons tamari or low-sodium soy sauce
½   cup all-fruit raspberry jam
1   teaspoon prepared mustard
1   teaspoon freshly ground black pepper

Rinse chicken and dry with paper towels. In a small bowl, combine soy sauce, jam, mustard, and pepper. Brush mixture on chicken. Put chicken into a 3 ½-quart slow cooker. Pour rest of sauce over chicken. Cover and cook on low for 5 to 6 hours or until chicken is tender; serve over brown or wild rice.

Note: You may thicken the juices with a mixture of 2 tablespoons cornstarch to 2 tablespoons water.

CROCK POT

SERVES 6   SWEET 'N' SOUR FIVE-SPICE TURKEY THIGHS

2	pounds boneless, skinless turkey thighs
½	cup green onions, chopped, including tops
2	tablespoons teriyaki sauce
1	teaspoon garlic powder
1	tablespoon rice wine vinegar
1	tablespoon raw honey
1	tablespoon dark molasses
1	teaspoon five-spice powder
1	teaspoon toasted sesame seed oil
¼	teaspoon white pepper
1 ½ to 2	tablespoons cornstarch
2	tablespoons water
1	tablespoon toasted sesame seeds (garnish)
½	cup thinly sliced green onions (garnish)

Trim meat of all visible fat and place in a 3 ½-quart slow cooker. In a small mixing bowl, combine onions, teriyaki sauce, garlic powder, molasses, honey, vinegar, five-spice powder, sesame seed oil, and white pepper. Stir well and pour over turkey. Cover and cook on low about 6 hours, or until turkey is tender. Remove turkey and add cornstarch and water to cooking juices, then cook on high for 15 to 20 minutes, or until thickened. Slice turkey, serve over brown rice pilaf, and sprinkle with sesame seeds and onions.

CROCK POT

POT ROAST MOROCCO WITH COUSCOUS

SERVES 6 TO 8

4	pound boneless pot roast
1 ⅓	teaspoons ground ginger
½	teaspoon turmeric
½	teaspoon cumin
½	teaspoon paprika
½	teaspoon freshly ground black pepper
	sea salt to taste
1	medium onion, sliced
4	parsnips
4	carrots
1	10-ounce package couscous, prepared according to directions

In a small bowl, combine ginger, turmeric, cumin, paprika, and pepper. Press into both sides of roast. Set aside while preparing vegetables. Put sliced onions on the bottom of a 4- to 5-quart slow cooker. Place seasoned beef on top of onions. Scrub parsnips and carrots and cut into 2-inch lengths. Place parsnips and carrots on top of beef. Cover and cook on low for 7 to 8 hours, or until roast is tender.

Serve pot roast and vegetables with the couscous.

CROCK POT

PASTA SAUCE WITH MEAT

SERVES 6

½   pound extra-lean ground round
½   pound lean ground turkey breast
2   stalks celery, finely chopped
2   medium carrots, finely chopped
2   cloves garlic, minced
1   medium red onion, chopped
1   28-ounce can diced or crushed tomatoes
1   6-ounce can tomato paste
1   teaspoon sea salt
2   tablespoons raw honey
¼ to ½   teaspoon freshly ground black pepper
½   teaspoon basil
1   teaspoon oregano
2   tablespoons fresh parsley, minced

Combine ground beef, ground turkey, celery, carrots, garlic, and onion in a 3 ½-quart slow cooker. Stir well. Then add tomatoes, tomato paste, salt, honey, pepper, oregano, basil, and parsley to pot and stir. Cover and cook on low for 7 to 8 hours, or until meat and vegetables are tender and blended well. Serve over whole wheat pasta or brown rice.

CROCK POT

CORNISH HENS WITH ROSEMARY

SERVES 3 TO 6

3	Cornish hens, thawed
¼	cup dried onion
3	tablespoons fresh minced rosemary (or 3 teaspoons dried)
2	tablespoons fresh minced parsley
½ to 1	teaspoon freshly ground black pepper
1 to 2	cloves garlic, minced, or 1 to 2 teaspoons garlic powder
1	teaspoon sea salt
1 to 1 ½	cups all-fruit grape or apricot preserves
2	bay leaves

Rinse hens and pat dry with paper towels. Cut the hens in half and season with dried onion, rosemary, parsley, pepper, garlic and salt. Place hens in 4- to 5-quart slow cooker along with the bay leaves and cook for 5 to 5 ½ hours on low, or until hens are tender. Then remove the hens and add grape or apricot preserves to the juices in the bottom of the slow cooker. Cook 15 to 20 minutes on high, or until juices are thickened. Drizzle sauce over hens and serve with wild rice, cooked with pine nuts or toasted almond slivers.

CROCK POT

SERVES 8 TO 10 BARBECUED BRISKET WITH ARTICHOKE LINGUINE

2 ½- to 3-pound flat-cut extra-lean beef brisket

1 ½	cup low-sodium catsup
2	tablespoons raw honey
1 to 2	teaspoons Liquid Smoke
1 ½	teaspoons hot horseradish
2	teaspoons mustard
⅛ to ¼	teaspoon cayenne pepper
	12 ounces artichoke linguine

Remove all visible fat from meat and place in 3 ½-quart slow cooker. In a small mixing bowl, combine catsup, honey, Liquid Smoke, horseradish, mustard, and cayenne pepper. Mix well and pour over brisket. Cover and cook on low for 7 to 8 hours or until brisket is tender.

Cook noodles according to directions. Rinse and drain. Slice meat against the grain and serve on top of noodles. Spoon sauce over all.

CROCK POT

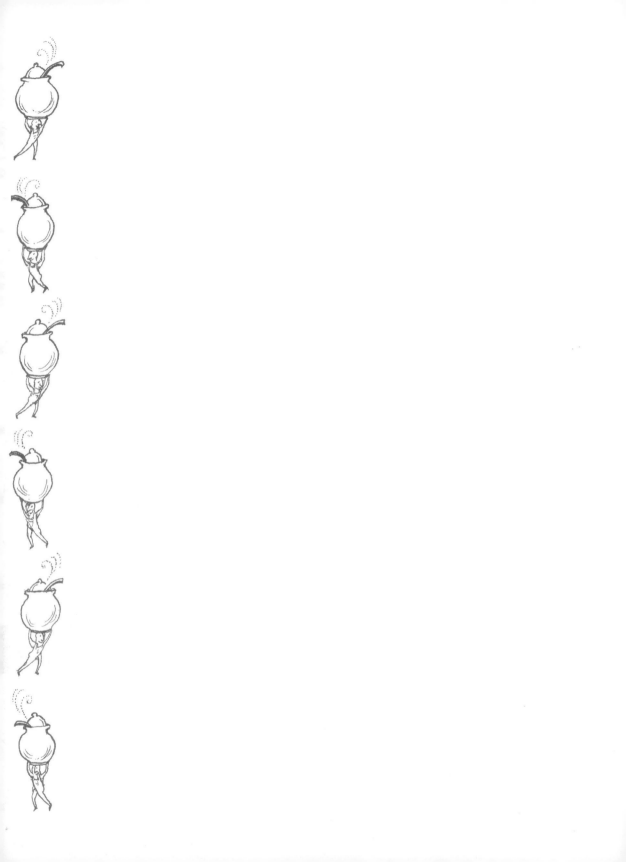

Chapter 16

Is It Soup Yet?

Nothing is more soothing on a cold winter day than a bowl of hot soup! Soup is great for weight loss as well because you feel full and satisfied. All of the following soups are low-fat and low-sodium, but they're full of flavor—so enjoy some soul-soothing soup without guilt.

PEA SOUP SERVES 8 TO 10

1	pound split peas
1 ½ to 2	quarts filtered water
1 ½	cups diced onion
2	teaspoons Liquid Smoke
2	cups diced carrots
1	clove garlic, minced
1	teaspoon oregano
1	teaspoon basil
	sea salt and freshly ground black pepper to taste
	Molly McButter Buds for serving

Rinse peas and place in large pot or Dutch oven. Add all other ingredients to pot except Butter Buds and cook 1 to 1 ½ hours. Add Butter Buds to each individual serving. Serve with whole grain breads or crackers.

Note: Lentils can be cooked the same way, with 1 teaspoon cumin and 2 cups diced potatoes in addition to all the other ingredients except peas.

SOUP

SERVES 4 TO 6

GAZPACHO

½ cup chopped celery

3 medium cucumbers, peeled, seeded, and diced

2 cups low-sodium chicken broth

3 large tomatoes, peeled and seeded

½ cup chopped green onions

1 cup diced green bell pepper

¼ cup fresh lime juice

½ cup diced jicama

2 tablespoons chopped cilantro

1 teaspoon sea salt

1 teaspoon cumin

½ teaspoon chili powder

2 tablespoons raw honey

¼ teaspoon cayenne pepper

1 cup tomato juice

1 avocado, diced

¼ cup toasted or curry pepitas

Combine in large glass or stainless steel mixing bowl all ingredients except avocado and pepitas; stir well. Chill in refrigerator for 1 to 2 hours before serving. Garnish with avocado and pepitas, and serve with baked, unsalted corn chips.

SOUP

ASPARAGUS POTATO SOUP

SERVES 4 TO 6

1 ½ to 2 quarts filtered water

3	cups chopped asparagus
3	cups grated raw potatoes (peel on)
½	cup chopped chives or green onions
4	tablespoons Molly McButter Buds
1	teaspoon tarragon
1	teaspoon sea salt
⅓	teaspoon cayenne pepper
1	clove garlic, minced
2	tablespoons pecorino or Romano cheese (garnish)

Combine all ingredients in a large pot or Dutch oven. Cook until potatoes have become infused throughout the mixture and the broth is slightly thickened. Adjust the seasoning if needed. You may thicken the soup further by using a cornstarch and water mixture or puree it in the blender for a creamy consistency. Garnish with freshly grated pecorino or Romano cheese and serve with whole wheat crackers or bread.

SOUP

SERVES 6 TO 8   VEGETARIAN VEGETABLE SOUP

HIGH FIBER/FAT-FREE

1 to 2 quarts filtered water
8 carrots, thinly sliced
4 parsnips, thinly sliced
5 stalks celery, diced
1 large red onion, diced
½ large head green cabbage, roughly chopped
2 to 3 cloves garlic, minced
2 bay leaves
sea salt and freshly ground black pepper to taste
2 cups salt-free diced tomatoes
4 tablespoons raw honey

Place all ingredients except and tomatoes and honey in a soup pot. Completely cover vegetables with filtered water. Cook over moderate heat until vegetables are tender to the bite. Add the tomatoes and cook for 5 minutes more, then add raw honey. Turn off heat, stir well, and serve. Keeps well for several days in an airtight container in refrigerator. Delicious reheated!

SOUP

CHINESE CHICKEN VEGETABLE SOUP

SERVES 10 TO 12

LOW-FAT/HIGH FIBER

6   hormone-free boneless, skinless chicken breasts
2   cups carrots, julienned
2   cups celery, julienned
1   cup diced white onion
3   cloves garlic, minced
1   cup bok choy, chopped
2   cups Chinese mustard greens, finely chopped
1   tablespoon rice wine vinegar
1   tablespoon toasted sesame seed oil
½   cup green onions, finely chopped (garnish)
½ to 1 cup coarsely chopped snow peas
    low-sodium soy sauce and white pepper to taste

Heat 3 to 4 quarts filtered water and 2 teaspoons sea salt in a large pot over high heat. When water reaches a boil, add chicken breasts. Skim water often during cooking so that broth remains clear. After the chicken is done, remove from pot and cut up into bite-size pieces. (Only 3 to 4 breasts are needed—refrigerate or freeze the others for another use.) Set chicken aside. Place carrots, celery, onion, and garlic in pot of chicken broth and bring to a boil. Add bok choy, Chinese mustard greens, and rice vinegar. Cook 5 minutes, then turn heat off. Add toasted sesame seed oil; stir in soy sauce and white pepper to taste. Add chicken, stir well, and serve garnished with green onions and snow peas.

SOUP

SERVES 4 TO 6 **CORN CHOWDER**

6 to 8 ears of corn
    4   cups plain rice milk
    2   tablespoons raw honey
    4   tablespoons Molly McButter Buds
    1   teaspoon garlic powder
   ½   teaspoon sea salt
        freshly ground pepper to taste
    1   tablespoon minced parsley

Cut the corn from the cob into a large bowl. Then take a spoon and scrape the entire cob to get the liquid. Coat a large skillet with butter-flavored nonstick spray and place over medium-low heat. Add fresh corn, milk, Butter Buds, garlic powder, sea salt, pepper, and parsley to pan and cook about 10 minutes, stirring constantly. The starch in the corn will have a tendency to stick and burn easily. When corn is almost done, add honey and stir well. Remove from heat and serve.

SOUP

FRENCH ONION SOUP

6	cups low-sodium beef broth
1 ½	cups thinly sliced yellow onion
¼ to ½	teaspoon freshly ground black pepper
½	teaspoon garlic powder
⅓	cup fresh grated pecorino cheese
2	cups oven-toasted croutons

Coat a skillet with nonstick spray and place over medium heat. Add onion to pan and cook until translucent and lightly browned. Heat beef broth in a large saucepan over medium heat. Add onions, pepper, and garlic powder to broth. Deglaze the skillet, scraping up any bits of browned onion, with a little more broth and add to saucepan. Bring just to a boil and let simmer 10 minutes. Serve in individual bowls with cheese and croutons.

SOUP

Note: Make croutons by cutting stale whole wheat bread into cubes. Place on cookie sheet, spray with butter-flavored nonstick spray, and sprinkle with a bit of garlic powder and sea salt. Bake at 400 degrees until golden brown and crunchy.

SERVES 2 TO 3   COLD AND SPICY TOMATO SHRIMP SOUP

3   cups unsalted tomato juice or unsalted V-8 Juice
1   cup cooked shrimp
     juice of 1 lemon or lime
1   teaspoon horseradish
1   tablespoon raw honey
2   tablespoons Molly McButter Buds
½   teaspoon garlic powder
¼   teaspoon soy sauce

Combine all ingredients in large bowl and add sea salt to taste. Chill in refrigerator before serving.

SOUP

Chapter 17

Fruit of Your Labor

Fruit is God's dessert for man to savor. It's sad that we've traded glucose for sucrose. The following recipes are designed to get you back to the natural glucose found in fruit. Fruit is full of vitamins, minerals, and natural fiber. It's a great snack food, especially for your children. I encourage you to always keep a big beautiful bowl of fruit on your kitchen counter.

Attention Princesses: Don't eat more than one piece of fruit per day while you're losing weight; preferably only 2 to 3 times a week.

👍 Eating for Excellence Food Tip:

FRUIT

Always eat fruit by itself. Wait at least an hour after any meal to eat fruit, or you will experience indigestion.

APPLES AND BANANAS

SERVES 4 TO 6

6 very ripe bananas, sliced
4 apples, thinly sliced
1 teaspoon cinnamon
½ teaspoon nutmeg
1 teaspoon pure vanilla

Coat a nonstick skillet with butter-flavored nonstick spray and place over medium-high heat. Place sliced bananas in skillet and stir until they begin to brown. Then add apples and mix together. Cook until the apples are tender when pierced with a fork. Stir in cinnamon, nutmeg, and vanilla at the last minute of sautéing. Spoon into dessert dishes and eat warm or cold.

Note: This is a delicious topping for nonfat or low-fat frozen yogurt or frozen Rice Dream.

FRUIT

HOMEMADE CRANBERRY SAUCE

SERVES 6

1	bag fresh or frozen cranberries
2	cups fresh pineapple, cut in 1-inch chunks
⅓	cup pineapple juice
1 ½	teaspoons orange zest
½	cup raw honey or ½ cup all-fruit jelly (orange/pineapple or cherry)

Place cranberries, pineapple, pineapple juice, orange zest, and honey or fruit jelly in food processor. Process until all cranberries have been crushed. Pour mixture into covered bowl and chill until ready for use.

Optional garnish: Crushed walnuts or pine nuts may be added right before serving.

FRUIT

BAKED APPLES

2 to 3   large, firm apples (rome and granny smith apples hold their shape
       well)

2   teaspoons cinnamon

½   teaspoon nutmeg

¼   cup crushed or slivered almonds or walnuts

1   cup raisins, soaked in hot water until plump

¼   teaspoon sea salt

⅓   cup raw honey

Preheat oven to 350 degrees. Use an apple corer to remove the stem and seeds of the apples. Place in a nonstick pan that has been coated with butter-flavored nonstick spray. In a small mixing bowl combine remaining ingredients. Spoon into center of apples. Bake apples until tender. Remove from oven and let rest a few minutes. Serve with vanilla yogurt or a fresh raspberry puree.

FRUIT

SERVES 4 TO 6   POACHED PEARS

½   cup water

2 to 3   pears, halved and cored

1   tablespoon fresh lime juice

3   tablespoons raw honey

1   teaspoon orange zest or 1 teaspoon minced fresh mint

1 to 2   cups low-fat vanilla yogurt

Place water in skillet on medium-low heat, then add pears, cored side up. Cover and cook for 5 to 7 minutes or until just tender. Remove from heat and add lime juice, honey, and orange zest or mint.

Combine yogurt with enough juice from the pears to thin the yogurt to a drizzling consistency. Whisk until combined and pour over pears. Serve immediately.

FRUIT

ALL TROPICAL SALAD

SERVES 6

2   cups fresh pineapple chunks
1   cup papaya chunks
1   cup mango chunks
1   cup sliced bananas
1   cup sliced kiwi

Combine all ingredients in large mixing bowl and fold gently until well combined. Chill in refrigerator in covered container until ready for use.

Note: Piña colada yogurt makes a nice topping for this salad.

FRUIT

SERVES 6 TO 8

GINGER PEACHY

8 large peaches, sliced
1 cup plain low-fat yogurt
1 tablespoon fresh grated ginger
1 teaspoon pure vanilla
½ cup low-fat cottage cheese
⅓ cup raw honey

Combine yogurt, ginger, vanilla, cottage cheese, and honey in a blender; pulse until smooth. Pour mixture over the sliced peaches and chill for 30 to 60 minutes. Stir well before serving.

FRESH FRUIT POPS

Berry Pops

2   cups strawberries, black raspberries, or blueberries

2   cups apple juice concentrate

½   cup bottled water

Tropical Pops

2   cups crushed pineapple

1   cup orange juice concentrate

½   cup bottled water

Combine fruit, juice, and water in blender or food processor and blend or pulse until pureed. Pour into freezer-pop molds and freeze overnight.

Note: ½ cup plain or flavored low-fat yogurt makes creamy fruit pops.

FRUIT

Chapter 18

Sweet Dreams

I chose this title for the chapter because I dream about desserts and I love treats. Here are some tasty desserts that do more than treat your taste buds; they treat your body to the goodness of natural sugars. We've already talked about the side effects of white sugar, so this is the good part of the book—dreamy desserts without the harmful side effects. Enter into excellence and have some sweet dreams.

 Eating for Excellence Food Tip:

Don't dream every day. Remember, the Bible says too much honey is not good for you. Just because it's healthy, that doesn't give us permission to give in to gluttony. Enjoy but don't be too sweet.

SWEETS

EVERYBODY LOVES JELL-O

SERVES 4 TO 6

But Jell-O has a lot of added colorings and preservatives. This is a very healthy alternative—and no one will never know the difference!

Knox unflavored gelatin
fruit juice
diced fruit

Prepare gelatin according to directions on the package, except use fruit juice and add fresh fruit (except for pineapple—used canned instead). Be sure to buy all-natural fruit juices at the health food store; they are superior in taste and don't have the added sugar of most juices in grocery stores.

Pour gelatin into a bowl, a mold, or a bundt pan and chill until firm. Serve and enjoy!

SWEETS

BROWN RICE PUDDING

SERVES 4 TO 6

2	cups cooked brown rice
2	cups plain rice milk or organic nonfat milk
4	hormone-free eggs
½	cup raw honey
1 ½	teaspoons allspice or five-spice powder
2	teaspoons pure vanilla
½	teaspoon sea salt
1	teaspoon Molly McButter Buds
½	cup raisins, soaked in hot water until plump

Preheat oven to 325 degrees. Combine all ingredients in a large mixing bowl and mix well. Coat a 2-quart casserole dish with butter-flavored non-stick spray. Pour mixture into dish; cover and bake for 40 to 45 minutes.

Cool to room temperature and serve immediately or chill before serving.

SWEETS

SESAME STICKS

SERVES 3 TO 4

1 ½   cups sesame seeds, unhulled
  2   tablespoons raw, unprocessed peanut butter
  ¼   cup chopped walnuts
  2   teaspoons pure vanilla
  ¼   teaspoon sea salt
  2   tablespoons organic barley, oat, or rye flour
  ¼   cup raw honey

Preheat oven to 325 degrees. Combine all ingredients thoroughly, then spread mixture evenly on a nonstick cookie sheet. Bake at 325 degrees for 10 to 20 minutes. Cut into stick shapes. Leave on cookie sheet to cool; sticks will harden as they cool. Lift them out carefully.

SWEETS

SERVES 6 TO 8

L.A. GRANOLA BALLS WITH DATES

1   cup toasted almonds
¾   cup chopped dates
½   cup raisins
½   cup filtered water
2   tablespoons raw, unprocessed peanut butter
1   teaspoon pure vanilla
2   cups L.A. Granola

In a grinder or food processor, grind toasted almonds until very fine. Place in a bowl. Combine dates, raisins, and water in a saucepan and heat until the mixture comes to a boil. Remove from heat and let rest for 10 minutes for fruit to soften. When mixture has cooled to warm, place in blender or food processor and blend until smooth. Add peanut butter, vanilla, and granola, then form into balls. Roll in bowl of ground almonds. Serve immediately or store in the refrigerator or freezer.

SWEETS

BASIC VANILLA SHAKE

2   cups vanilla Rice Dream
1   teaspoon pure vanilla
1   tablespoon raw honey
1   cup ice (more if needed)

Place all ingredients in blender and blend for 1 to 2 minutes to the desired consistency. Pour the mixture into beautiful glasses or goblets.

Note: You may add 1 tablespoon toasted oat bran or a scoop of protein powder for extra fiber.

SWEETS

SERVES 2

VAN-ORANGE DELIGHT

1   cup freshly squeezed orange juice

1   cup plain nonfat yogurt or Rice Dream

¼   cup orange juice concentrate

½   teaspoon pure vanilla

1 to 2   cups ice

Place all ingredients in blender and blend to desired consistency. Pour into glasses and enjoy.

Note: Pineapple or any tropical fruit juice may be substituted for the orange juice.

SWEETS

ALMOND CHOCOLATTE

SERVES 2 TO 3

1	cup almond milk or rice milk
1	cup chocolate Rice Dream
1	teaspoon raw honey
1	teaspoon almond flavoring
1 to 2	cups ice

Place all ingredients in blender and blend to desired consistency. Pour into glasses and enjoy.

SWEETS

SERVES 4 TO 6

THAT'S THE RASPBERRIES

1 cup plain nonfat yogurt
2 tablespoons all-fruit raspberry jam
1 ½ cups fresh or frozen raspberries
1 teaspoon pure vanilla
½ cup vanilla Rice Dream
1 to 2 cups ice

Place all ingredients in blender and blend to desired consistency. Pour into glasses and enjoy.

SWEETS

PEACHY KEEN

SERVES 2 TO 3

1	cup vanilla Rice Dream
1	cup plain nonfat yogurt
2	cups fresh or frozen peaches (not canned)
1	tablespoon raw honey
1 to 2	cups ice

Place all ingredients in blender and blend to desired consistency. Pour into glasses and enjoy.

Note: Mangos, papayas, or pineapple can be substituted for the peaches.

SERVES 2 TO 3   TUTTI-FRUITTI

1	cup cranberry-apple or cherry cider all-fruit juice
1	banana
1 ½	cups fresh strawberries
1	tablespoon raw honey
1	cup vanilla Rice Dream
1	cup plain nonfat yogurt
1 to 2	cups ice

Place all ingredients in blender and blend to desired consistency. Pour into glasses and enjoy.

SWEETS

FRUIT JUICE SPARKLERS

Reeducate your taste buds—these are healthy and delicious alternatives to soft drinks.

¾   cup sparkling mineral water
¼ to ⅓   cup pure fruit juice of choice
           squeeze of lemon or lime

Combine water and juice and pour over ice. Top with a squeeze of fresh lemon or lime juice.

Some of my favorite juices are raspberry-cherry and pineapple; cherry cider is a winner with children.

SWEETS

For more information about Sheri Rose Shepherd's
conferences, teaching tapes, and booking information, contact:
Foundation for Excellence
Post Office Box 3500, Suite 227
Sisters, Oregon 97759
1-888-777-2439

Index

INDEX

INDEX